Flight of the Westwind

Flight of the Westwind

By Russ Protentis

Copyright

Printed in the United States of America by Ingramspark

First Printing **April 2021**

ISBN **978-1-7362146-2-6** (**Print**)

ISBN **978-1-7362146-7-1** (**eBook**)

JEBWizard Publishing
37 Park Forest RD.
Cranston, RI 02920
www.jebwizardpublishing.com

JEBWizard Publishing
Books with Character

Dedication

This book is dedicated to all those brave soldiers and law enforcement officers who have given their lives to preserve the freedoms and law and order we continue to enjoy today, and for a country that allowed me to serve and protect the Greatest Nation God hath created.

Russ Protentis

Table of Contents

Prologue

Sitting in a Danbury Federal Correctional Facility cell, former Naval aviator turned convicted drug smuggler Tony Nargi wondered where he had gone so wrong.

A Naval Academy graduate, a skilled fighter pilot with at least two confirmed air-to-air combat victories against sophisticated Soviet MiGs over the skies of North Vietnam, recipient of a Silver Star and two Distinguished Flying Crosses for gallantry in combat, a rising star in the business world, Tony's once-promising life seem destined to wither away in a federal prison cell.

While Nargi served his time, Russ Protentis was just beginning his career as a federal agent. He was ambitious, intelligent, and committed to taking on new challenges. Protentis set his heart and soul into fighting the war on drugs.

In what might seem an unlikely series of events, Tony Nargi and Russ Protentis would join forces in a common purpose.

Nargi would have an opportunity to rehabilitate his honor. Protentis would have the chance to capture one of the country's most wanted fugitives and make the largest seizure of Colombian Cartel cocaine from a private aircraft in U.S. history.

Both would face enormous odds.

Nargi, the genuine danger of being discovered by the cartel and the vicious retribution they would visit on undercover operatives. Protentis, the resistance of an organization unaccustomed to proactive investigations and the potential harm failure might do to career ambitions.

They would combine skills—Nargi's combat aviation background and Protentis' investigative drive—to penetrate the cartel's organization on their home turf, risking it all for very different reasons.

The story had its beginning with one young man watching B-29 bombers returning from World War II and another exchanging a youthful dream of being a professional athlete for the more realistic, albeit more dangerous, life of a federal agent.

Splash one MiG

Summer, 1968

Off the coast of North Vietnam

Painting by Lieutenant (Ret.) Alex J "Rattler" Rucker.,

USN

Beginnings

In 1968, Navy Lieutenant Tony Nargi and his wingman, Lt. Alex Rucker, engaged in aerial combat against six enemy MiG fighters; three MiG-17s and three MiG-21s.

Outnumbered but confident in their abilities, they engaged the enemy putting all their skills and training to the test.

These are the moments of a fighter pilot's dreams, but only if they survived. Otherwise, they are the things of nightmares.

*****

Tony Nargi

On the run in to the intercept of the MiG's, we accelerated to about 450 knots, calculating this was the best compromise between speed and fuel burn. I was glad it was Alex on my wing. He was an excellent pilot who didn't lose his focus in a demanding situation.

As we sped toward the intercept turn, Red Crown informed us there were six MiGs (three MiG-17s and three MiG-21s). We stayed in constant communication with Red Crown during our missions, the call sign for a U.S. Navy guided-missile cruiser providing radar cover

1

for U.S. fighter jets over North Vietnam. As we would say in the fleet, "a target-rich environment." We were outnumbered three to one, but it never entered our minds. We were Navy fighter pilots; what difference did the odds make?

The MiGs were deployed with the 17s low and in front and the 21s high and behind. They were using the 17s as bait. If we targeted the 17s, when we completed our intercept turn, we would be behind the 17s but below and in front of the 21s, perfect targets for the trailing enemy aircraft.

We approached the MiGs head-on but offset when Red Crown started us into the intercept turn, a 180-degree turn to starboard. This turn would put us at the 17s six o'clock in firing position for our missiles or closing for a gun attack. We still did not have a clear tactical picture, unaware we were taking the bait and would soon be cannon fodder for the 21s. But Red Crown did. The controller realized we were being lured into a trap by the 17s and ordered an immediate hard port turn.

I didn't want to make that turn.

My chance of shooting down a MiG was being

taken from me. Even worse, I was turning my six o'clock toward the potential fight. But we turned immediately, training over instinct. The controller then reversed the port turn to a starboard turn. When I rolled out of the turn, I saw a MiG-21 slightly high at ten o'clock about 4,000 feet ahead..."

Surviving the battle in the skies was a culmination of training, equipment, skill, and mostly luck, lived by Nargi, his wingman, and the pilots in the MiGs. The terror in the skies would last but a moment. The thrill would last a lifetime. Perhaps the addiction to the adrenaline of a life and death uncertainty would send Tony on a trajectory he'd never imagine himself following.

Life had a few surprises ahead for Lt. Tony Nargi, but first, he had to deal with the MiG 21 in his sights.

POTUS and Naval Training

On July 3, 2000, U.S. Customs Special Agent Russell Protentis stood onboard the USS Intrepid Aircraft Carrier Museum's flight deck anchored at its berth on the Hudson River New York City. Assigned to assist the United States Secret Service on a protection detail for President of the United States. Protentis mingled with other agents on the Intrepid's deck as they awaited Bill Clinton and his wife for a pre-Fourth of July celebration. The museum staff busily prepared the flight deck of the floating museum for the President and First Lady.

Protentis was one of a few hundred U.S. Customs agents assigned to assist the U.S. Secret Service, detailed to provide security for the President and other foreign dignitaries during Operation Sail 2000. A celebration in New York City for the week of July 3rd.

While walking the flight deck of this floating Navy museum with other agents, Protentis happened upon an F-8 C Crusader fighter jet. Inscribed in black under the canopy was the name of the pilot, Lieutenant Tony Nargi.

Memory synapses fired off, bringing up the not-sodistant past when Protentis and Nargi forged an interesting association.

To the left of Nargi's name was a red star. Inscribed inside that star were the symbols "MiG 21" and dated 9-19-68. Protentis knew the history behind this Vietnam War Era fighting machine and the pilot he had developed a unique relationship with during the late 1980s. Back then, Nargi often discussed his experiences as a naval aviator in the Vietnam War and shooting down the enemy fighter.

Tony Nargi

I wanted to be a pilot. I never wanted to be anything else. From my earliest memories, in the late summer of 1945, at age five, when my father took me from our home in northern New Jersey to watch the B-29 bombers returning from Europe and landing at Teterboro Airport near our house, I was hooked.

Watching the airplanes planted in me a burning desire to fly. I had an uneventful childhood and graduated with a C average from high school. I would not set the academic world aflame. I still wanted to be a pilot, but I knew it was an impossible dream.

My father left school at age 12, apprenticed by his

father as a plumber, then became a truck driver, and in 1947 a plumbing and heating contractor.

He wanted me to be an engineer, preferably in the construction industry. He believed that becoming an engineer was the mark of success in life. Having little choice, I became a freshman at Newark College of Engineering.

NCE was a New Jersey state school with an excellent reputation yet would accept a C-average high school graduate.

If he was from New Jersey.

I would live at home and drive to and from school daily. After the first two weeks of classes, having not understood most of what the professors were trying to teach, and not having the nerve to tell my parents that engineering was not for me, I kept driving back and forth to school every day, just not attending classes.

At this time, my parents took their first vacation, driving to Florida. I was spending Saturday on the porch of my cousin-in-law's home, who lived next door and retired from the Navy because of a heart condition. He mentioned he had read in the paper that the local Congressman was giving a competitive exam for appointments to the service academies. There were three slots available for the Naval Academy, two for the Military Academy, and one for the Air Force Academy.

My cousin suggested I take the exam. I laughed. I took the exam and scored first out of 300. No one was more surprised than I. You had to select which academy you were applying to before the exam. I chose the Naval Academy because it had three slots.

It didn't matter. I knew nothing of the academies except I always rooted for Army during the annual football game. There were six appointments to the Naval Academy, three primary and three alternates if a primary candidate failed to qualify.

Four applicants failed to qualify, and only two of us reported to the Naval Academy in July 1959. The letter from the Congressman's office giving me a primary appointment and the letter from NCE inviting me not to return arrived the same day. My father got to them first.

His reaction? 'I don't know whether to kiss you or kill you.' I was the only one to survive plebe year and graduate in June 1963. I knew the Academy was my last chance at being something more, so I worked as hard as

I could and finished about the middle of my class.

My third year at the Academy was when I discovered Navy pilots flew Navy aircraft, and not U.S. Air Force pilots. The Navy had the second largest air force in the world after the USAF.

The dream was alive.

Before graduation, you had to choose which part of the Navy you wanted to join. I chose Naval Aviation, flunked the flight physical, and got assigned to a destroyer in the Pacific.

It crushed me, coming so close to my dream.

While in training, I injured my back, requiring surgery. The surgery disqualified me from operating an aircraft. It also made the drive from Annapolis, Maryland to San Francisco, California, long and depressing.

I reported for duty and discovered that the ship was in the Hunter's Point Naval Shipyard in San Francisco for three months for retrofitting (upgraded and repaired). While the ship was in dry dock, the officers had no responsibilities other than determining what to do with the rest of the day after breakfast. Mostly we went to the officer's club for Bloody Mary's and lunch, then drove to downtown San Francisco for the rest of the afternoon and evening.

At six feet, one inch, and 185 pounds, I was the third smallest officer of the fifteen on the ship. None were fat; they were just enormous. My first few months in the Navy did not bode for an exciting time.

Retrofit complete, we left the shipyard for sea trials. During these trials, among other aspects, tactical Navy aircraft would simulate attacking the ship. This would test the accuracy of our gun directors. On this day, the Officer of the Deck was the ship's executive officer or XO, as we called him. I was junior Officer of the Deck.

As we finished this trial, the aircraft made a low pass by the ship before departing. As they flew past, I must have had a wistful look on my face.

The XO said, "I couldn't help noticing the look on your face."

This led to a discussion of my wanting to be a naval aviator but flunking the flight physical. The XO told me he had been a Naval aviator but had turned in his wings. He volunteered to get me an appointment with a flight surgeon he knew at the Naval Hospital. The next time we returned to port, he arranged a meeting.

At the flight surgeon's office, I explained I had a back operation because of a football injury as a plebe at the Naval Academy that disqualified me from flight training. He instructed me to strip to my underwear and lie on the gurney. I did, and he took a rubber-headed hammer, reversed it, and scraped the handle along the sole of my bare foot. He asked if I could feel that and if it hurt.

I replied I could feel it. And no, it didn't hurt. He did the same thing to the other foot; same questions, same replies. I would have replied in the same way had the pain been excruciating. I wanted to be a pilot.

I returned to the ship confident that I was now physically qualified for flight training.

The next day I received my orders. I had ten days to drive from our home port in Long Beach, California, to Naval Air Station, Pensacola, Florida, for flight training. I figured if I drove non-stop from California to New York, spent five days with the love of my life, Joanne Patricia Regan, who lived in the Bronx, New York, then drove without stopping from New York to Pensacola, I could do it all in ten days. I took fifty-six hours to go from California to New York non-stop.

I don't remember how long I took to drive non-stop from New York to Florida, but I arrived in time for check-in at Naval Air Station (NAS) Pensacola.

Just in time.

My roommate in flight school was another ensign and Academy classmate named Willie Gentile. Willie was from New York and had a steady girlfriend also from New York whom he planned to marry. He talked incessantly about his girlfriend and their upcoming marriage. I never tired of listening to his plans. We got along well. His girlfriend decided not to marry him. She was unyielding in her decision. Willie developed many strategies and schemes to win her back.

All to no avail. His marriage talks convinced me I should get married. After proposing by mail, I got married the following April. Fifty-five years later, we are still married and have three children, two boys and a girl, and eight grandchildren.

The Navy had a system where after primary flight training—consisting of thirty-two hours of airborne instruction, solo flights, and classroom training—the first student in the class got to choose what intermediate pipeline he would go, jet, prop, or helicopter. The selection went on down the line to the last student in the class.

I was first in my class, but there were no slots available in the jet pipeline which I wanted. I was forced to choose between propeller planes and helicopters. I reported to Naval Aviation School (NAS) Whiting in Milton, Florida, near Pensacola, where I would receive further instruction in the T-28, a single-engine propeller-driven aircraft with a tandem cockpit. The prop intermediate pipeline trainer.

After our wedding, Joanne and I moved into a trailer park in Milton. Again, I was first in my class after completing the syllabus. The Intermediate Prop Pipeline's last step was to carrier-qualify in the T-28 aboard the USS Lexington, then off Pensacola's coast. This required six carrier landings, which we had been practicing at outlying fields. After qualification, I returned home.

Joanne and I then left in our car, a 1963 MGB, that we had packed the night before, for NAS Corpus Christi in Corpus Christi, Texas, where they assigned advanced pipelines. We had six days in which to make the trip. We drove through the night in a torrential downpour, arriving in Corpus Christi at five o'clock in the morning the following day.

We checked into a motel where I left Joanne and headed for the base. I got to the base at approximately 6:00 A.M., parked the car, and walked through the driving rain to the administration building to check in.

By the time I arrived, I was soaked, and the only person there was a Navy Chief. I explained to him why I was there. He looked at me as if I had two heads but said the Detailer—the officer who would assign advance pipelines—wouldn't arrive until eight o'clock.

For almost two hours, I sat there, dripping on the floor until there was a good size puddle beneath me. At eight o'clock, the Detailer arrived, strode by me, and went into his office. After a few minutes, the Chief said, 'You can go in now, sir.' I went into the Detailer's office, and he invited me to sit down.

"Are you the officer who was sitting in a puddle outside my office," he said.

"Yes, sir, I was here to check in for advanced training."

"When did you finish intermediate training?" he

asked.

"Yesterday, sir."

"You know you have six days to check-in. You could have gone to the exchange and bought yourself an umbrella."

"I want the jet pipeline, sir," I said.

"Well, if you graduated from the Intermediate Jet Pipeline at Meridian, it should be no problem."

"I went through the Intermediate Prop Pipeline at NAS Whiting, sir."

"Then you can't switch from the Prop Pipeline to the Jet Pipeline."

"But, sir, I was first in my class at Pensacola when there were no jet seats at Whiting. I was first in my class again at Whiting, and I want to fly jets."

"Is that true?" he said.

"Yes, sir."

He then gave me orders to the Advanced Jet training center.

They assigned me to Pipeline at NAS Kingsville in Kingsville, Texas, 46 miles south of Corpus Christi. I rushed to the motel to tell Joanne. I was elated.

I wanted to go see the airplane I would fly next, the

F-9 Cougar jet, so we hopped in the MGB and drove to Kingsville. When we got to the base, I didn't want to go out to the flight line, so we went to find an F-9 in a hangar.

We did, and we walked over to the aircraft. I climbed up the side for a close look at the cockpit. I recognized nothing except the stick and the throttle, and they barely looked familiar. All of my newly found confidence evaporated. I could never fly this aircraft. The advanced jet training syllabus had two aircraft, the F-9 and, after that, the final thirty hours of flight training in the F-11 Tiger.

I didn't want to see an F-11, as I was sure I wouldn't get that far. We moved into base housing, and I began the advanced jet syllabus. I worried needlessly. The F-9 was easier to fly than the T-28. I relaxed somewhat and enjoyed the flying. That was a mistake. My progress through the advanced syllabus went well until we reached the air-to-air gunnery phase in the F-11.

I listened attentively to the instructor's briefing.

In the exercise, there was the tow aircraft with the banner we would shoot, four shooters, one of whom was the instructor leading the flight. We flew to the range. I was number three. With it my turn to shoot, I rolled in from the perch. Before shooting, I realized my firing gun was not operating, and I could not fire. I turned to parallel the tow aircraft's flight path.

When I rolled out to look for the tow aircraft, it was not there. I saw no other members of the flight either. I radioed the instructor advising him.

I had lost sight of the flight. The instructor told me to return to base.

During the debrief of my performance, I was the first topic of dialogue. It went something like this:

Instructor: "You flew as if you had never been in a gunnery pattern before."

Me: "I haven't, sir."

Instructor: "Didn't you receive gunnery instruction in the T-2 at Meridian?"

(Meridian, Mississippi was the home of the Navy Intermediate Jet Pipeline, flying T-2 aircraft, a single-engine tandem cockpit jet trainer.)

Me: "I didn't go to Meridian, sir; I went through Whiting."

The instructor said nothing. Finally, he said, "Report to me at 0800 tomorrow morning, and I'll tell you what we've decided". Convinced they would send me to the advance prop pipeline, or worse, send me back to a ship in the surface fleet, I waited in dread.

They did neither.

Instead, they gave me additional ground and flight instruction in air-to-air gunnery and then returned me to the standard syllabus.

I completed advanced training and received orders to VF-174 at NAS Cecil Field, Florida, near Jacksonville. VF-174 was one of several Replacement Air Group (RAG) squadrons.

This one operated the F-8 Crusader, a single-seat single-engine jet fighter with four internal 20 mm cannons carrying 200 rounds of ammunition and air-to-air missiles, rockets, or bombs.

Their mission here was teaching newly winged pilots how to fly and fight in the F-8. I had made it! I had my pilot's wings of gold. I would be a Navy fighter pilot, and I received my first orders. I would be flying the F-8 Crusader onboard the USS Aircraft Carrier Intrepid.

And headed to Vietnam.

Ejection: Losing a Plane, Learning a Lesson

Flying is always a challenge. Flying in combat presents a whole different set of challenges, but that doesn't mean training is not without risks.

As his Navy career continued, Nargi received orders for his second combat tour. Before he returned to Vietnam, he had to survive bailing out of a damaged fighter and plunging into the ocean off the Florida coast.

Tony Nargi

It was a beautiful day in Norfolk, Virginia, as the USS Intrepid launched from the naval base, destined for the South China Sea. Onboard the carrier was a new Air Wing. Only two of the pilots had combat experience. My first combat cruise aboard the USS Oriskany in 1966 made me one of them.

I was part of a detachment of fighters from Fighter Squadron 111 onboard the Intrepid to protect the bombers from MiGs as they completed their missions. My home port was at NAS Miramar in San Diego. If you saw the movie "Top Gun," NAS Miramar became the base for the Navy Strike Fighter Tactics Instructor Program in March 1969.

As the ship sailed along the Florida coast, due to the Air Wing's scant combat experience, the Air Wing Commander held a rehearsal Alpha Strike against one of the many practice military targets in Florida.

A section—consisting of two fighters, a lead and a wingman—were assigned to the strike group. After our catapult shot, I joined and climbed to 20,000 feet, the altitude at which the joined bombers were proceeding to the target. Because of the delay in our launch, we were well behind our assigned position in the strike group, so I advanced the throttle to gain more speed.

As I moved the throttle, the engine unwound and stabilized at about three percent below idle. Not enough to remain airborne.

I turned toward the ship as we were about 70 miles from the coast, so any help would come from the carrier.

I tried everything to get the engine to respond to throttle movements. Nothing worked; ejection became my only option. As I glided toward the ship, I experienced a strange phenomenon. I always thought, once I decided my only option was to eject, apprehension would kick in. Instead, it was like I was sitting next to another pilot preparing to eject, watching with interest but not connected.

I rolled down my flight suit sleeves, put on my gloves, threw my knee pad on the top of the instrument panel, fastened the other side of my oxygen mask, and put down my visor. I turned toward Carl on my wing, kissed him off, positioned myself in the seat, and ejected.

We had the older version of the Martin-Baker ejection seat equipped with a five-inch cartridge and requiring 120 knots of forward speed and a level attitude. I didn't know then, but the Martin-Baker seat had never lost a pilot who ejected within the envelope and even saved some who ejected outside the envelope. I was the 2,000th ejection in the seat's history.

When I pulled the handle above my head, the canopy separated from the aircraft, and the seat fired. I tumbled forward, and the drogue chute deployed, stabilizing the seat. Then the main chute deployed, separating me from the seat, leaving the survival gear and the raft strapped to me.

The survival instructions appeared clearly in my mind.

First, throw away the oxygen mask. This was in case the pilot lost consciousness. There were about ten minutes of oxygen in the emergency bottle. If the pilot were still unconscious after they depleted the oxygen, the oxygen mask would suffocate him. I then checked the chute deployed above me, twenty-four feet of white silk, a beautiful sight. I inflated my Mark 3C, which was flotation gear we wore around our waists.

After inflation, I pulled the handle at my hip and deployed the survival gear, inflating the raft.

I could now turn my attention to the sea below me. As I descended, all I saw were white caps. Waiting until my boots hit the water, I released the chute.

The chute blew ten or twenty feet from me before settling into the water. I went about two or three feet below the surface before rising, retrieving the raft, and climbing aboard. I looked around and saw the rescue helicopter, but it was heading away from me. It was dark. Reaching into the survival pack, I retrieved a flare, ignited the smoke end, and held it aloft.

As the rescue helicopter approached me, I fired

another smoke flare which gave him wind direction for the hover. He faced into the wind, hovered, then lowered the rescue sling, a distance of about fifty feet from the helicopter to the surface of the sea,

The helicopter pilot must lower the rescue sling into the water before the pilot reaches it to discharge the static electricity buildup. Failing to do this, when the pilot touches the sling, the static electricity charge will kill him.

When the rescue sling hit the water, I dove into the ocean, swimming toward the sling, a distance of less than 100 feet. I got about halfway there when my forward progress stopped. I thought, here I am within fifty feet of the rescue helicopter and about to drown when one of the helicopter crew shouted out, "The raft is strapped to your butt."

Embarrassed, I pulled out my knife and cut the lanyard.

My ego wounded, they hoisted me aboard the helicopter, and we began the short flight back to the ship. A brief discussion between the pilot and me, capped by a promise of a Jack Daniels bottle, ensured my raft incident would not become part of the official accident report. The aircraft lay in pieces at the bottom of the ocean, and we never determined the cause of the problem.

The carrier continued around the southern tip of South America on its way to the northern coast of Vietnam. Carriers never went through the Panama Canal because they didn't fit. It would also trap them, unable to launch aircraft to defend themselves—easy prey for an enemy.

The carrier arrived off the coast of North Vietnam and started combat operations. It surprised most that, except for the apprehension on the first few missions, it was like a continuance of training—until the first enemy contact.

Surviving has little to do with skill so much as luck. Being shot down is as much being in the wrong place at the wrong time as it is pilot skills.

The Intrepid Air Wing acted much like air wings before it. On the first few missions, mistakes happened. But, if a pilot got through his first nine or ten missions, his chances of surviving the cruise increased.

The lure of combat is irresistible until the reality of violent death hits you. Most dealt with death by injecting humor into the situation. This habit has gotten me into trouble over the years, but it is still how I deal with the ever-present specter of death.

I vowed that just flying the F-8 in combat would not be the highlight. I had led my fighter squadron on several successful bombing runs into enemy territory. Our well-trained squadron developed a sterling reputation as having never lost a bomber or fighter jet on any mission.

On August 1, 1968, while engaged in an aerial conflict with several bandits (MiGs), I spotted some U.S. fighter jets, flying just below me, under attack by eight bandits.

I vectored additional units from the Intrepid to the location where they would stave off the MiGs' attack while myself and other aircraft from our squadron continued to engage our original targets. I had expended my Sidewinder missiles, which missed their targets, then found myself headed directly toward a MiG-17 at two o'clock. The MiG was also out of missiles.

I had about 100 rounds remaining in my 20 mm cannon and had to be accurate. Closing on each other, I fired a burst of rounds at the bandit as he fired back at me. I then released a second burst which struck the target. Seeing smoke from the tail area of the aircraft confirmed the hit. I didn't destroy the MiG but put him out of the fight.

Within seconds the entire group of bandits fled for home, but not before one U.S. fighter chased and took down the wounded MiG.

We were victorious!

I received a gold star to acknowledge a second Distinguished Flying Cross. I was proud of contributing to downing the MiG, but I still wanted to take down my first enemy aircraft, alone, one-on-one. I had complete confidence in my ability as a naval aviator and looked forward to the next conflict.

Facing the Enemy

By the end of the summer of 1968, Tony had led his fighter squadron on many successful bombing runs into enemy territory. He vowed to maintain the squadron's reputation for never losing a plane on any of their missions.

Tony Nargi

It was another humid, sultry day anchored in the South China Sea off the coast of North Vietnam. Waking up bright and early and heading topside, the smell of diesel fuel and saltwater permeated the flight deck of the USS Intrepid. I wondered what challenges would lie ahead.

The day began routinely, considering that, for an hour or two, the enemy might try to kill me as we tried to kill them.

There were various means at their disposal to accomplish this task; small arms fire, anti-aircraft cannons, surface-to-air missiles, and occasionally MiG-17 and MiG-21 aircraft. The Russian-manufactured MiG is an abbreviation derived from the names of its designers Artem Mikoyan and Mikhail Gurevich. They were, in the hands of a skilled pilot, formidable aircraft.

The U.S. had its own arsenal of weaponry, including bombs, rockets, missiles, guns, and aircraft. Each side was only partially successful, and tactics on both sides evolved as countermeasures improved. Our pilots never went below three thousand feet to avoid small arms fire. They constantly maneuvered the aircraft to disrupt the fire control solutions of the anti-aircraft cannons. Lessons learned at a high cost in blood and hardware.

Tony's wingman this day was Lt. Alex "Rattler" Rucker, and they had an easy day. Rather than go overland with the bombers to defend against MiG attacks, they were assigned Barrier Combat Air Patrol, BarCAP. The mission placed them between the aircraft carrier and the beach if the enemy attacked the vessel.

Since this was an unlikely scenario, it meant they bored holes in the sky for about an hour and a half before returning to the ship. The one break in the boredom came when they reached almost half the fuel load. They would meet up with a KC-135 tanker, refueling in the air back to full.

The more internal fuel aboard, the better the chances of winning an engagement. Little did they know that the mission would change shortly after refueling, and the extra fuel would prove handy.

Their controlling agency, Red Crown—the call sign for a U.S. Navy guided-missile cruiser that provided radar cover for U.S. fighter jets over North Vietnam—detected MiG airborne activity over the beach and sent Tony and Rucker a vector to intercept.

Every U.S. Navy fighter pilot fantasizes about outmaneuvering an enemy aircraft in a confrontation and then shooting it down. Victory in aerial combat against enemy aircraft is the zenith of the profession. This was the reward for all the years of training, cruises, and extended family separations.

Every fighter pilot woke up each day, hoping this would be the day. For "Rattler" and Tony, this was their day, a once-in-a-lifetime opportunity. Success would validate them as Navy fighter pilots, the best in the world.

Failure could mean death.

Would they trade our profession for any other? Not a chance. Losing an engagement to an enemy never crossed their minds.

Tony Nargi

While turning to head in the direction provided by
Red Crown, I advanced the throttles to full military
power, just short of afterburner. It is a feeling like no
other, invincibility, strength, control.

I was flying an F-8C Crusader aircraft, a single-seat
single-engine Navy fighter carrying four 20 mm
cannons with 200 rounds of ammunition and two AIM
9D Sidewinders. They could carry four Sidewinders,
but the additional weight lowered the aircraft's
performance to an unacceptable level.

If the aircraft were in a dogfight, or hassle as we
called it, the pilot wanted all the performance he could
get. In training, we most often flew F-8 against F-8,
which meant the pilot knew the performance of the
opposing pilot's aircraft intimately and exactly how
much fuel it carried.

The pilot's skill—and the better he understood his
aircraft's performance — determined the winner. Most
F-8 against F-8 hassles ended in scissors or rolling
scissors (a low-speed tactical maneuver,) which meant
the lowest and fastest aircraft had the advantage.

We used afterburner sparingly, mainly to

accelerate after a hard turn and regain speed quickly. While it dramatically increased thrust, it used an enormous amount of fuel. How fast a fighter goes impresses civilians, how tight it turns, and how quickly it regains speed after the turn impresses pilots.

On the vector to intercept, we were devoid of emotion, neither elation nor fear. I was performing the tasks for which I trained efficiently. As though written in bold on the windscreen.

On the run to intercept the MiGs, we accelerated to about 450 knots, calculating this was the best compromise between speed and fuel burn. I was glad it was Alex on my wing. He was a good pilot who didn't lose his focus in a demanding situation.

As we sped toward the intercept turn, we stayed in constant communication with Red Crown. They informed us there were six MiGs—three MiG-17s and three MiG-21s—within our range.

As we would say in the fleet, 'a target-rich environment.' We were outnumbered three to one, but it never entered our minds. We were Navy fighter pilots. What difference did the odds make?

The enemy deployed the 17s low and in front and

the 21s high and behind. They were using the 17s as bait. If we targeted the 17s when the intercept turn was complete, the attacking aircraft would be behind the 17s but below and in front of the 21s, perfect targets for the trailing enemy aircraft.

We were now flying deep into enemy territory near Vinh Son, North Vietnam. Approaching the MiG's head-on but offset when Red Crown started us into the intercept turn, a 180-degree turn to starboard. This turn would have us arriving at the 17s at six o'clock, the firing position for our missiles or closing for a gun attack.

We still did not have a clear tactical picture and were unaware we were taking the bait and would soon be cannon fodder for the 21s. But Red Crown did. The controller realized we were being lured into a trap by the 17s and ordered an immediate hard port turn.

I didn't want to make that turn. My chance of shooting down a MiG was being taken from me. Even worse, I was turning my six o'clock toward the potential fight. We turned immediately.

Training over instinct.

The controller then reversed the port turn to a starboard turn, and when I rolled out of the turn, I saw a MiG-21 slightly high at ten o'clock, about 4,000 feet ahead. It was a near-perfect day for flying with a broken cloud layer at 10,000 feet and visibility above the broken cloud layer unlimited. I saw the target silhouetted against a clear blue sky.

The MiG-21 maneuvered, confirming that he saw me. I calculated the best tactical move he could make was a turn into me, heading directly for me and converting his altitude advantage to speed.

Instead, he started into a loop, giving me the tactical advantage. It allowed me to get behind him and follow him in the loop. When we completed the maneuver, I had closed to about 3,000 feet at his six o'clock. He turned left, and I realized he did not see me.

Reversing his turn, turning right, trying to find me, he passed directly in front of me. I had a solid tone emitting from the missile's nose as it locked on an infrared heat source , the enemy aircraft engines.

He reversed his turn. When he was about wings level, I fired one of my AIM 9D Sidewinder missiles. The missile tracked and flew beside the port fuselage of the MiG-21. It detonated near the port wing root and severing the tail of the aircraft from the fuselage.

As the tail broke into pieces, flames enveloped the rest of the aircraft. The canopy popped open, and the pilot, Vu Dinh Rang, ejected. His white and orange paneled parachute opened, and he began his descent to the ground.

As I was savoring the moment, it lulled me into a near-fatal mistake, focusing on the downed MiG. The sound of Alex's voice broke my concentration, piercing my headset.

Look out! You have a MiG behind you.'

I looked back, and there was a MiG-21 about 2,500 feet behind. My heart raced. The MiG had fired a missile headed directly for me.

The MiG-21 can carry up to six air-to-air I.R. tracking missiles, not as good as our AIM 9D's, but good enough. It also carried an internal 23 mm twin-barrel cannon with 420 rounds of ammunition. In the hands of a trained pilot, this was a deadly weapon.

I had no choice and immediately went to idle, dropped the speed brake (a device designed to slow the aircraft quickly), and executed a high G barrel roll. One G being the force of gravity on a pilot's body during flight. A high G barrel roll instantly helps slow the aircraft by increasing G to over six and changes its flight direction.

Alex told me to break right. I immediately slowed from almost 500 knots to about 150 knots. The missile missed. It should have destroyed my aircraft. As I saw it fly by, I was elated. I thought the enemy pilot would convert his almost 350-knot speed advantage to altitude, then roll in for another missile or gun attack.

Instead, he did the unthinkable. He flew in front of me, firing his cannon as he went by. I was a ripe target, out of airspeed and ideas. Again, he missed me.

Realizing his mistake, he dove to 10,000 feet, heading into a broken cloud layer about 5,000 feet below us. I immediately raised the speed brake and went to afterburner, following the MiG. I selected the second missile, got a tone indicating tracking, and fired. I rushed the shot as he approached the cloud layer, and he turned and defeated the missile.

Alex got a good tone and fired one of his AIM 9D Sidewinder missiles. It tracked perfectly to the MiG and detonated at its tailpipe. Still, the damn thing kept on accelerating away and shortly climbed into the overcast.

We never knew if the missile was tracking the MiG or the I.R. emissions from the clouds, which also emit heat, causing it to detonate. The remaining four MiGs scattered and ran for home. Our squadron had downed one MiG and was hungry for more, but we didn't have enough fuel to give chase.

Alex and I rendezvoused and headed for the Intrepid. My emotions overwhelmed me as the blood pulsated through my veins. I had done it; I reached the pinnacle of my chosen profession.

When we arrived at the Intrepid, Alex 'trapped' (we called this an arrested landing.) I made a high-speed flyby at deck level, then ended the maneuver with a vertical rolling climb indicating an aerial victory. I then trapped, cleared the arresting wires, and taxied forward to my parking spot on the bow.

There was a crowd waiting for me, including the Skipper of the ship and a special visitor, four-star Admiral John S. McCain, Jr., father of the late Senator. The Admiral's son was then a prisoner of war. Admiral McCain was the commander of all U.S. forces in the Pacific. We chatted and had our picture taken.

A fitting end to an exhilarating day of combat.

The Path Less Taken

Russ Protentis

As a young man attending West Junior High School in Brockton, Massachusetts, I set my sights on becoming a federal agent.

Back then, I had two distinct goals. First, I would continue my junior high school baseball career that would launch me to the Major League, where I would play for the Boston Red Sox.

My second, and more practical goal, was to become an FBI agent. I grew up watching the television series *The F.B.I.* starring Efrem Zimbalist Jr. Captivated by armed agents dressed in sport coats and ties, chasing and capturing bank robbers, hijackers, and organized crime figures, I resolved to become one of them.

At Northeastern University, I enrolled as a Criminal Justice Major. I chose Northeastern because of their cooperative education program, a five-year program including at least one year of fieldwork in your major.

In my freshman year, I set the groundwork for my future. During my first meeting with my Cooperative (Coop) Education advisors, David Hammond and Jean

Burns, they told me there would be several opportunities to find a paid Coop opportunity. These would be available the following spring and summer with a variety of federal agencies.

I hadn't abandoned my baseball career; the siren's song of the majors still called me. Fall tryouts for the freshman baseball team were on my agenda. If I made the cut, they would invite me to continue into spring tryouts. Continuing to pursue my career paths—baseball and the FBI—I looked forward to what the future would bring.

I made the fall cut for the freshman baseball team, and they invited me to continue in the spring. I was one step closer to Fenway Park.

In December, I met with my primary Coop coordinator, David Hammond, who said he had some good news and bad news. The good news was that the Federal Bureau of Alcohol, Tobacco, and Firearms (ATF) would hire a Coop student for the spring quarter. The bad news was that they sought a female for the position because of the workplace climate and need for diversity in the agency. Mr. Hammond said he would send three females and three males for the interviews the following week and wanted to know if I was interested.

I said, "Yes."

It was not the FBI, but it was still an opportunity to work

for a federal law enforcement agency. I had never heard of ATF, but I would make it my goal to become familiar with their mission.

The following day, I went to the JFK Building in Boston, MA. Taking the elevator to the 17th floor, I found the office of the Special Agent in Charge of the Bureau of Alcohol, Tobacco, and Firearms. I spoke with the receptionist, told her I was doing research on ATF, and asked for any literature available.

She directed me to a bookshelf near the office entrance handing me several pamphlets which included information about some of the agency's high-profile investigations.

During the next few days, to prepare for my interview, I studied and committed to memory the contents of the literature. The big day arrived. Dressed in my only suit, I traveled by subway to the JFK Building for my interview, reviewing the literature on the ride.

Entering the reception area, the woman I had spoken to the week before remembered me.

"Are you the young man I gave all those pamphlets and literature to last week?"

I nodded.

"Are you the last student here from Northeastern University?"

"I think so," I said.

She led me into a large conference room and introduced me to the Special Agent in Charge (SAC), Arthur Montouri, and the Assistant Special Agent in Charge (ASAC), John Ennis.

The conference room walls seemed to close in as I entered. I took my seat on the opposite side of the large oak table. Montouri spoke first.

"So you want to be an ATF agent?"

"Yes, sir," I answered.

"We would like to start with one question if you don't mind."

My heart was beating so hard I felt it would burst through my chest as my mind raced in a million directions.

"Please, sir."

Ennis asked, "What do you know about ATF?"

Expecting something different, I repeated the question, "What do I know about ATF?"

"Yes, son," Montouri said.

I exhaled. For the next 15-20 minutes, I recited the complete chronology of ATF's history, jurisdiction, and highlights of the agency's most recent high-profile investigations.

As I finished speaking, Montouri said, "Someone has

done their homework."

Ennis added, "You are the first person we have interviewed that took the time and effort to investigate our agency."

"Young man," Montouri said, "our special agents investigate federal crimes, and you seem to have a great aptitude for investigating."

I had nailed the interview. Both Montouri and Ennis said I impressed them with my presentation but were restricted by their Headquarters mandate to hire a female for the next Coop Position in the spring.

However, they told me another position would open up in the summer, and they would hire me with no further interviews. Also, Ennis said he would inform Dave Hammond and Jean Burns they had selected me to fill the vacancy in advance for the summer position.

Montouri congratulated me and shook my hand, while Ennis said he would give me a tour of the office. I would begin my paid Coop job with ATF in June as an administrative staff employee. Mr. Ennis told me I would earn overtime whenever I went out with agents on nights and weekends.

I realized it was time to hang up my baseball cleats. I met with the coach the following day, and he replied with a phrase I later learned was from the book of Proverbs.

"When you become a man, you put childish things away."

I thanked him for his counsel, returned to my dormitory room, and neatly packed my baseball glove and cleats in a box.

The spring semester had just ended, and while my dormitory friends headed home for the summer, I prepared for my position with ATF.

My first week there, I must admit, was rather mundane administrative work. I spent my time reviewing multiple purchases of firearms by the same individuals or tracing the ownership of a firearm recovered by a local or state police department, but I lived for the after-hours work.

I would have done it for free!

I loved the job, conducting surveillances of undercover buys, going with agents on interviews, volunteering for any assignment available. The agents in the office appreciated my enthusiasm and alerted me to any assignment I could participate.

A few agents gave me a call sign for the mobile radio communications system, identifying me as ATF 5000., Completing the ATF Form 5000 to start a trace on a firearm used in a crime or recovered during an investigation by a local or state police agency was my primary responsibility. As the program's temporary coordinator, I would trace the history of the firearm ownership all the way back to the manufacturer.

At the end of my Co-op term with ATF, a few agents I worked with took me out to a local pub for a sendoff party.

I could not wait to return!

However, on the 4th of July weekend 1976, I received a telephone call from Mr. Ennis asking me if I wanted to return part-time, voluntarily, while attending classes. I agreed. I met with Ennis on Monday, July 5th. He told me I received a secret security clearance before my first rotation after a background check.

Government security clearances come in three levels, confidential, secret, and top secret. Having a secret security clearance would give me access to sensitive critical investigative information.

It was heady stuff for a college kid.

He asked if I had seen the news of the recent terrorist bombings in Massachusetts and New Hampshire. A group of domestic terrorists was wreaking havoc on coastal New England sites, detonating homemade incendiary devices at targeted government locations. He asked if I wanted to assist in the investigation, he would get authorization from Northeastern University for me to work with ATF during the investigation.

I signed a release document and reported to ATF after class the following day.

During a briefing with other ATF agents from Boston and dozens of agents from out of state temporarily assigned to the FBI, I learned that a radical prison reform group—demanding changes to the U.S. Prison system—claimed responsibility for the bombings.

They designed these attacks to receive maximum attention during the bicentennial anniversary of the U.S. Independence from Great Britain. The first bombing occurred in April 1976 at the Suffolk County Courthouse in Boston, MA, injuring twenty-two people, including a man who lost a leg.

Eleven explosions occurred in coastal New England, most during the July 4th weekend, damaging an Eastern airlines commuter plane, several government buildings, and National Guard Armory in Dorchester, MA.

None of the explosions resulted in a fatality.

My assignments were simply to assist other ATF agents in surveillance activities. The investigation led to the indictment and arrests of several domestic terrorists less than ten days later.

After two weeks of assisting the ATF agents on weekends and after classes during this investigation, Mr. Ennis thanked me for my help. I returned to academic life until the winter of 1977, when I began my second Coop tour at ATF.

On my return for a second co-op tour, Mr. Montouri told me there was a freeze on hiring in the federal government, but when they lifted it, I would become a Special Agent in the Boston office.

On May 14, 1977, I finished my last term at Northeastern University and graduated cum laude with a 3.75 GPA. I now had 120 days of non-competitive eligibility for hiring by ATF with no test or examination.

However, if the government didn't lift the freeze before the 120-day period passed, I would have to compete for a position like anyone off the street. I was enjoying my post-graduate summer at the beach and traveling the country.

Sixty days of my eligibility passed without the U.S. Government lifting the hiring freeze.

I had a few calls from Mr. Ennis. He was doing his best to create an opening for me. My mom, who always pushed me as a teenager, told me to get off my ass and write letters about my predicament to my representatives in Congress.

I drafted a letter explaining the obstacle in my pathway to my lifelong career goal of becoming a federal agent. I sent a copy to Tip O'Neill, Speaker of the U.S. House of Representatives, Senators Ed Brooke and Ted Kennedy, and President Jimmy Carter.

On days 95 through 100 of my eligibility, I received form letters from O'Neill, Brooke, and Kennedy saying they knew about the hiring freeze and were resolving the issue.

The letter from President Carter's office was much more encouraging. His staff, the letter explained, were researching the issue and would resolve it in my favor.

On day 116 of the freeze, around 9:30 in the morning, I received a letter from the Office of President of the United States, 1600 Pennsylvania Ave. Washington, DC. I scrambled to open the envelope.

To my surprise, the letter said they would lift the freeze on federal hiring for one day to allow me and several others to begin a career with the federal government. My dream of becoming a federal agent became real.

The letter, signed by President Jimmy Carter, showed him to be a man of his word. The President had made it happen.

At 11:30 am, on the same day, I received a telephone call from a very irate Arthur Montouri, SAC ATF in Boston. The man who interviewed me for my co-op job.

"I have a letter on my desk from the Office of the President of the United States," he said, an edge to his voice. "I want you to hear me good. I worked to get you hired in my office. This letter has nothing to do with your employment. We don't like letter writers," he paused. "Understand something, I was responsible, not the President!"

I apologized. and thanked him repeatedly. I knew he wanted me to massage his ego. He told me my reporting date to the office would be September 12th. I expressed my gratitude and hung up. I wrote a thank-you letter to the President, not knowing I would thank him face to face three years later.

In 1977, I was sworn in as a Special Agent with the Bureau of Alcohol, Tobacco, and Firearms. From 1977 through 1981, while with ATF, I conducted several intriguing investigations and presented the first federal arson for profit case to the U.S. Attorney's Office in Boston.

In 1980, while investigating an interstate gun case, I developed an informant who introduced me to a gun runner making silencers for handguns. The subject of this investigation worked in a machine shop and built a prototype attachment that would silence the sound produced by a handgun.

Under federal law, the illegal possession of a silencer was punishable by 10 years in prison. After two successful undercover purchases of silencers from an individual I knew only as Willie, he introduced me to Luis Pascal, who would offer to sell me several firearms stolen from a residence in New York.

My first undercover meeting with Pascal went well, and we met in a public area later in the day to do the deal. As I left the rendezvous location, while stopped in traffic, another agent who had been surveilling the meeting pulled alongside my undercover vehicle and asked me to roll down my window.

I looked in my rearview mirror. Pascal was in his vehicle two cars behind me. I ignored the agent's motions and continued forward, but Pascal followed the agent as he turned onto a side street.

Had this compromised me? I would soon discover. I

called the informant, who said Pascal was still ready to sell me the firearms and we should meet again in Bellingham Square in Chelsea, MA.

At 5:00 PM, I met with agents from my office assigned as backups for the undercover meeting with Pascal. I arrived in Chelsea and parked my undercover vehicle on Broadway. A few moments later, Pascal greeted me on the sidewalk and asked if I could follow him to another location where he would sell me the guns.

"Not until I see the guns," I said.

Pascal insisted I follow him, and I continued to refuse. I noticed another individual coming up behind me. Within seconds, I was on the ground beside my undercover vehicle. Pascal, a Golden Gloves boxing champion, struck me on the jaw, sending me tumbling back over his partner who had ducked behind me.

I lifted Pascal onto my shoulder and pinned him against my vehicle, then struck him several times. Finally, my back-up team arrived and handcuffed Pascal and his associate.

I went with other agents to the Chelsea, MA Police Headquarters with blood spouting from my jaw. My boss, Jack Dowd, told me Pascal's associate was on federal parole after a conviction for selling two kilograms of cocaine to an undercover Drug Enforcement Administration (DEA) agent.

I thought he would make a great witness, but my supervisor let him go. It would prove to be an enormous mistake.

One officer involved, a detective with the Chelsea Police Department, said Pascal was in a holding cell with one hand cuffed to the wall. He handed me a baseball bat and told me I should use it during my interview with him. It might be the only justice he'd get, the detective told me.

Tapping the bat in my hand, I looked at Pascal for a moment, letting the idea roll around in my brain, then decided I would let a jury decide his fate.

At Boston Medical Center, I received fifteen stitches on my jaw, but my foremost concern was my surgically repaired neck. An MRI revealed the attack might have caused another herniation of a disc in my neck.

In 1978, I ran surveillance of my partner, who was working undercover, making a purchase of a stolen firearm in Fall River, MA. As the investigation's target passed by my vehicle, I slouched down in the front seat to avoid detection.

When I straightened up, I heard a loud pop in my neck, followed by a sharp pain in my shoulder. I lost the sensation in my right arm and hand, resulting from a ruptured disc in the C5-C6 region of my spine.

In June 1979, I had surgery to remove the damaged disc

and a fusion of the C5 and C6 vertebrae. This is the area injured during the attack by Pascal. I still suffer the painful effects of nerve damage to this day.

Pascal's trial for assault on a federal agent in U.S. District Court did not result in the justice I had hoped for. A new jury sitting on their first trial heard testimony from Pascal's ten friends saying they had seen me strike him first.

After my testimony, the jury took one day to decide the verdict. Guess who they believed? Had my supervisor taken a witness statement from Pascal's associate, who was on federal parole and unable to avoid cooperating, he would corroborate my testimony before the jury. The outcome might have been different. I learned a valuable lesson about jury persuasion.

In 1981, on an assignment attempting to locate a wanted federal fugitive, the results of an attack on me would have different results.

On a balmy July afternoon in 1981, Special Agent Mike Dawkins (aka Doc) and I caught an assignment to locate a federal fugitive. While watching the fugitive's girlfriend's home, a large, bearded man approached my side of the vehicle.

The man, standing about 6'3", weighing over 250 pounds, knocked on my window. As I rolled down the window, he said he had information for me, and without warning, his fist came flying through the opening and struck me on the cheek.

In a fit of rage, I flung the door open, knocking him backward. As he rose to his feet, I struck him with the handle of my firearm, sending him sprawling over trash cans in the yard. Regaining my composure, I placed his wrists in handcuffs.

Louis Crescenza, the guy who'd assaulted me, was an associate of the fugitive we were trying to locate. He had a lengthy criminal record, including three arrests for assaulting a police officer. This case would be different. This time I had a witness.

Dawkins called my supervisor, who advised us to turn Crescenza over to local police. We transported him to the Revere Police Department in Revere, Massachusetts, charging him with assault and battery of a police officer. Crescenza, who'd had many confrontations with law enforcement, said he "hated cops."

Two weeks later, the Assistant District Attorney prosecuting the case said Crescenza would plead guilty to the charges and accept a sentence of eighteen months in state prison.

Crescenza gave me the address of the fugitive now living

in New Hampshire. I agreed to the sure thing, avoiding the risk of a trial. My office later presented me with a plaque engraved to Russell "Rocky" Protentis, which remains in my home office to this day.

Just another day in the life of an ATF agent.

Created in 1972 by Executive Order, the primary responsibility of BATF is to investigate violations of federal firearms, tobacco, alcohol, and explosives laws. As an agency under the U.S. Treasury Department, ATF also has the primary responsibility to assist the United States Secret Service in protecting presidential candidates and foreign dignitaries.

The Secret Service had limited resources to provide security for all the Presidential candidates during an election campaign. Secret Service trained agents from other Treasury Department agencies to bolster their numbers to assist in protection details. The United States Secret Service most often called upon agents from the Internal Revenue Service, U.S. Customs Service, and Bureau of Alcohol, Tobacco, and Firearms to assist in this effort.

It was Columbus Day in October 1980 and the home stretch of the presidential election campaign. The U.S. Secret Service needed ATF agents to assist at several locations in Boston. I was assigned to the Knight of Columbus (K of C) in the North End of Boston, where President Carter would speak as an honored guest.

On arrival, Secret Service site coordinator, Special Agent Peter Grant, assigned me to a post outside the holding room and inside the hall. President Carter came into my area with his Presidential Protection Detail. The security detail leader told us the President would pause in the hallway to greet several VIPs before entering the holding room.

Within seconds I was an arm's length from the most powerful leader in the world.

After greeting several luminaries, the President hesitated at the doorway to the holding room. "Good morning," he said, nodding to the other agent and me. I had my opportunity, so I took my only chance.

"Good morning Mr. President and I want to thank you."

He paused for a moment and replied, "For what, son?"

The other agent motioned for me to stop talking.

"I wrote a letter to your office during the hiring freeze, and you lifted it. That's why I am here."

He smiled. "Your welcome, son."

His detail now took control of the hallway and moved me to the walkway in front of the building. I would now have my back to him when he exited the building, and we would never meet face to face again.

The President left twenty minutes later. I focused on my job, identifying any potential threat to the President. His detail passed by me on the way to the waiting motorcade. It was the highlight of my young career to thank the man who made it possible.

Another assignment with the Secret Service would also shape the future of my career as a federal agent. In the summer of 1980, I was assigned to a protection detail in Concord, New Hampshire for presidential candidate and Governor of California, Ronald Reagan.

It was disturbing to hear a candidate for the President of the United States promising a group of NRA members he would reduce the size and authority of ATF. Soon after his election President Reagan, after speaking at another NRA conference, fulfilled his pledge.

Within a few months, I received notification from Martin Ward, Director of the Personnel Department of ATF, that I might be a victim of downsizing during the next several years.

During this time of uncertainty in ATF, my brother Paul was dating the daughter of Alfred DeAngelus, the Deputy Commissioner of the U.S. Customs Service. The DeAngelus family was rooted in Cranston, Rhode Island.

At a family gathering, my brother overheard the Deputy

Commissioner discussing the possible recruitment of ATF agents by the U.S. Customs Service. After hearing this, I asked my brother to approach Mr. DeAngelus about my interest in joining the United States Customs Service. Mr. DeAngelus was very receptive to the idea and advised my brother to informed me to contact him in his office in Washington DC.

I had purchased a home, recently married my wife Lynda—who was pregnant with the first of our five children—and was concerned about job security with ATF.

I heard rumors the United States Customs Service was interested in hiring 200 agents nationwide from ATF. Part of their effort to gain experienced agents to enhance their role in the "War on Drugs." To survive as an agency, with help from Senator John Glenn, ATF received authority to investigate arson for profit. Still, it wasn't enough to stop agency downsizing.

Mr. DeAngelus and I had a charming conversation. He asked me if I would be in Washington, DC soon. I told him I would try my best to meet with him.

Once again, divine intervention would play its hand in my future.

ATF in Boston had taken the lead in a massive arson investigation in the city of Lynn. The fires destroyed several commercial buildings and caused millions of dollars of destruction in its wake. After days of rummaging through the rubble for evidence of arson, other ATF agents and I gathered evidence of an accelerant used to fuel the blaze.

My supervisor was seeking a volunteer to bring these evidence samples for processing to ATF in Washington DC. I volunteered. The following day, I would be off to Washington with the evidence and a chance for a one-on-one interview with the United States Customs Service Deputy Commissioner.

I contacted Mr. DeAngelus. He said I could stop by his office anytime to discuss the possibility of my transition to his agency.

I arrived in Washington DC with a duffle bag containing eight aluminum paint cans, each filled with ash-charred pieces of wood and debris from the remains of the city block decimated by this massive blaze. After securing the evidence at ATF Headquarters, I walked to U.S. Customs Headquarters to meet with Deputy Commissioner DeAngelus.

The meeting went as planned. He said because he was Italian, he was not part of the U.S. Customs Service Office's political clique in Boston. He would do his best to place me there, but he would have to play politics with Tip O'Neill's

Irish Mafia in Boston. Two weeks later, the U.S. Customs Service Office in Boston contacted me and told me to report there for duty.

This career change set the stage for my full engagement in the war on drugs and meeting Tony Nargi.

Career Opportunities

Selling Planes to the Shah of Iran to Smuggling Drugs

After leaving the Navy, Tony worked for ten years for a defense contractor in the United States, which manufactured aircraft for the U.S. military. As he rose through the company's ranks, he took over sales of U.S.-manufactured aircraft to Europe and the Middle East, including Iran.

The relationship between the United States and Iran was as good if not better than most European Nations. The Shah of Iran was the proponent of a diverse and prosperous culture. Still, there was a definite caste system within the population. Tony's responsibilities in the Middle East took a significant hit as Iran's situation took a rapid downturn.

After completing the sale of nearly 100 U.S.-manufactured military aircraft to Iran, they ordered him out of that country. The fall of the Shah and the rise of Ayatollah Khomeini cast a pall over the country. It would no longer be a friend of America.

The assault on the U.S. Embassy and taking American hostages by the new regime, under the guise of a student uprising, ended U.S.-Iranian relations.

Tony's three children attended an English-speaking school, but his oldest son was entering high school. Joann, Tony's wife, wanted their son to further his studies back in Vermont. His family packed their bags and returned to New England to safely watch Iran's violent regime change.

While he continued selling U.S.-manufactured military aircraft to Europe, Tony had bigger ideas. He thought he would apply the technical expertise learned in the Navy and business acumen developed in international sales to establishing his own company.

In late 1980, Tony and two friends started a business in the Caribbean incorporating a twist on a trending vacation model, applying time share ownership to yachts in the Caribbean.

They believed this novel idea, with the proper capital, could be an instant success. But could never find that one solid investor with the money to adequately finance the operation. The business struggled.

Having drained their bank accounts and sold off assets trying to fund the company, they searched for alternative methods to prop up their failing business venture.

The partners—Tony's brother Paul and his brother-in-law, Joe Parisi—hit on a lucrative but risky idea. They would smuggle drugs from the Caribbean and South America into the United States.

After discreetly spreading the word that their business could supply transportation for drugs to the United States, Tony was introduced to a marijuana smuggler, Eddie Parker, from Massachusetts.

Parker, a slightly built man with brown hair, had purchased a load of marijuana in Jamaica and needed to transport the product to Vermont. Tony offered his services as a pilot, arranging for a leased aircraft. Parker and Tony traveled to Jamaica. He introduced Tony to the supplier, inspected the marijuana, and checked out the runway.

The landing strip restricted the size and range of the aircraft. The trip would require refueling at a coastal field in North Carolina, both on the journey to Jamaica and on the return trip to Vermont. The trip logistics would need as much planning and skill as a combat mission over North Vietnam.

Tony was back in his element.

He found a suitable aircraft in Pennsylvania—a Beechcraft Baron twin-engine passenger plane—and a company to install an additional fuel bladder tank to extend the range. The leasing company approved a one-year lease with monthly installments to begin thirty days after taking possession of the airplane. The financial arrangements were helpful for an unemployed pilot.

Planning in the style of a military mission, Tony plotted out the locations of radar along the east coast of the U.S. Calculating where he would need to fly below the radar coverage, manage the refueling stop, and navigate to the target landing location in Jamaica to avoid drawing attention to the aircraft.

Tony Nargi

I would treat this as a mission into enemy territory. My brother-in-law, Joe Parisi, and I would take-off from Burlington, Vermont, land in Wilmington, North Carolina, refuel the aircraft, and then head for Jamaica.

Out over the Atlantic, I would descend to 50-100 feet above sea level to avoid radar detection. Once beyond the U.S. territorial border of twelve nautical miles, I would climb to altitude and cruise until descending to Jamaica's runway approach.

On the return trip, as we approached the U.S., I would follow the same pattern to avoid radar detection. After refueling again in Wilmington, NC, we took off for Vermont. My brother Paul would meet us at a hangar at the Burlington Airport, transfer the marijuana into a van, and then secure the aircraft inside the hangar.

We'd use the cash from the first flight to pay the initial installment on the aircraft loan and accrue enough profit from subsequent runs to pay off the loan on the airplane.

I'd made it simple, uncomplicated, and precise. All seemed in order.

The basic strategy did not change for the other trips. I planned to remain in the smuggling business until we successfully restructured the Yacht Time-Share business. But, as in a war, when the bullets fly, the first thing abandoned is the plan.

Joe and Paul removed the passenger's seats from the airplane, reducing the aircraft's weight and increasing the cargo space. Plan in place; we were ready for the first flight.

On March 28, 1983, Joe and I buckled into the cockpit, filed a flight plan for Wilmington, North Carolina, and took off on our first mission to become millionaires. After a smooth flight over the Atlantic along the U.S.'s eastern seaboard, we landed as planned and refueled in Wilmington, North Carolina.

I warned Joe I would fly at a low altitude to avoid radar. I knew the adrenaline rush of low altitude flying. Joe didn't have that same experience. I told him to buckle up tight; I didn't want him bouncing around the cockpit, throwing off the aircraft balance.

After clearing U.S. territorial waters, we climbed to altitude. As we passed the east end of Cuba, we transferred fuel from the bladder tank. With the fuel now in the main tank, we headed to Jamaica's southwest corner and quickly found the makeshift landing strip.

Touching down, we taxied to the end of the strip near a small shack, repositioned the aircraft for takeoff, then shut down the engines. A pickup truck pulled up carrying several 55-gallon fuel drums with attached hoses and refueled the aircraft.

A second crew of five or six men removed thirteen fifty-pound bales of marijuana tightly wrapped in plastic from the shack and loaded the cargo on board. My heart raced. I had done nothing like this in my life.

Our time on the ground seemed like a dream. We were in a foreign country loading our plane with contraband that could lead to our arrest or worse. I did not see myself as a drug smuggler. I was a family man amid a financial crisis transporting relatively harmless material, albeit contraband, into the United States.

If something went wrong, how would I explain this to my family? Would they come to my rescue? These things roiled my mind as I watch the marijuana being loaded aboard the plane.

The Jamaican ground crew spoke English. They were quick and efficient. They were like a small, trained army on a mission of their own. We were back aboard in less than ten minutes, restarting the engines.

The leader of the crew said he hoped we would meet again soon. We taxied down the makeshift runway and took off for North Carolina. Looking back down on Jamaica, I could finally exhale as we headed back to familiar territory.

Flying at low altitude, we transferred fuel about halfway between the east end of Cuba and North Carolina. This was a critical point. Unlike the trip to Jamaica, with an empty aircraft, we had several places we could land if the transfer failed.

Now, loaded with marijuana, if we couldn't transfer the fuel, we would have to ditch at sea. I was familiar with the Naval Base at Guantanamo Bay (GITMO) in Cuba, having landed there frequently during my time in the Navy. If I landed with a planeload of drugs, I would face the wrath of Cuba and the United States, branded a drug smuggler and a traitor.

Even if we survived the ditching, no one knew where we were, so no one would look for us. Our chances of survival were slim.

The biggest obstacle in a fuel transfer was tank pressure. We had to wait until the fuel in the main tank was low enough so the transfer pump could overcome the tank pressure. Joe and I decided getting caught with a planeload of marijuana was better than being eaten by a shark.

We crossed our fingers, said a brief prayer, and the transfer worked. I breathed a sigh of relief. As we approached the territorial waters of the U.S., I began my descent to the deck, 50 feet above sea level, to avoid detection by radar.

After successfully penetrating the U.S. border, I climbed to altitude then contacted the airport tower in Wilmington, North Carolina, for landing instructions. They cleared us for landing, and we faced the next major obstacle. On the ground to refuel, we were vulnerable.

Nowhere to run, nowhere to hide.

Would there be an army of law enforcement officers waiting to whisk us off to prison for smuggling drugs?

We landed without incident and taxied to the refueling station, not a police officer in sight. Joe and I wiped the sweat from our brows, and I shut down the engines. The attendant came out to greet us. Joe rushed out to hand him his credit card. The last thing we wanted was for the attendant to get a look at our cargo.

We worried if the attendant got close to an opening in the aircraft, he would get a whiff of the sweet smell of Jamaican weed. The attendant took Joe's credit card and refueled the aircraft.

Once he finished refueling the plane, the attendant wished us a safe journey, and we took off for the last leg of our mission. We would be home in a few hours, the riskiest and most challenging part of our smuggling venture behind us.

Our landing at Burlington International Airport around 9:00 PM was a piece of cake compared to the last two landings. We taxied to the rental hangar where my brother Paul was waiting with a van.

The area was dimly lit. We had little concern about off-loading the fifty-pound bales of marijuana into the van. We had done it. Mission accomplished.

Paul drove, and Joe and I went along to make sure everything went smoothly. Parker rented a house on the base of a hill in the outskirts of Burlington. We parked the van in the driveway and walked up the stairs to the front door.

There was no need to knock.

Parker was partying with friends, the smell of marijuana permeating the air. The three of us walked into loud music and a bunch of stoned Vermonters. One of the male guests, stumbling to greet us, grabbed Paul's arm and asked if he wanted a hit off his blunt.

"Excuse me?" Paul said. This, if you knew my brother, was a bad sign. The guy removed his hand from Paul's arm, then made the fatal error of drooling on his new jacket. Paul looked at the wet spot on his left arm and, as I had often seen, landed a right cross squarely on the guy's jaw, sending him sprawling across the room.

I guess we now had everybody's attention. Parker

came running to meet us. Parker, several of his friends, and Paul, Joe, and I quickly off-loaded the bales of marijuana into the house. A few of Parker's guests, stoned out of their minds, said they could stay high for at least a year.

I told Parker to get our money; we didn't want to hang around there any longer, fearing the imminent arrival of local police. He returned with a paper bag containing almost fifty thousand dollars. It would cover the monthly cost of renting the plane, any related expenses, and leave a little for us.

I knew the thoroughness of our planning made for a successful mission. Parker asked me to fly to Miami in a few days, where he and I would plan a second trip. I traveled to Miami a few days later. We met at the airport, then drove to his home on the Inter-coastal Waterway.

He told me he would contact me once everything was ready in Jamaica. Parker asked if our plan needed any changes. I told him everything worked on the first trip as planned and saw no reason to change anything. On the drive back to the airport, Parker said he would call me in a few weeks to confirm our departure date.

I had the sense Parker had prior convictions for drug smuggling. He was cautious about our business and only discuss details in person. I did not have his phone number, and he would call me on a public telephone. The fuel transfer point on the return flight troubled me; it made us too vulnerable on the ground. But I didn't share this concern with Parker because I had no way to change it.

Joe, Paul, and I were ready for the second flight at a moment's notice. We were all eager to accrue profits. There were risks in everything; I just hoped I'd done everything I could to minimize them.

About ten days later, Parker called me.

'Ready for our next trip down south in two days?' he asked.

I told him we were, then met with my crew and planned our trip. In two days, a Thursday, the weather would be perfect. Everything looked good for another profitable run. Had we known what would happen on the second flight, we would have gotten out of the drug business for good.

On the morning of April 14, 1983, Paul drove Joe and me to the airport. We pushed the plane out of the hangar and topped off the fuel. I contacted the tower and filed a flight plan for Wilmington, NC. We were off again for Jamaica.

We landed right on schedule and refueled. After refueling, I contacted the tower for permission to take off on a sightseeing trip off the coast of North Carolina. After taking off and approaching the U.S. territorial border, I dropped the aircraft to 100 feet above sea level to avoid radar; we cruised for fifteen minutes and then climbed to altitude.

The flight was smooth, with little or no turbulence. As we passed the east end of Cuba, we transferred fuel from the bladder tank, then headed to Jamaica's South-West corner. We approached the strip from the same direction as before. A nice smooth landing and taxi ended this first leg.

As we waited for the approaching ground crew, I heard the distinct sound of gunfire. Bursts of machinegun fire. Shouts and angry voices. Adrenaline coursed through my veins. I planned the flight like a military mission, not knowing I would land in a war zone.

The leader of our supply gang rushed to the aircraft

as we ducked for cover under the plane. He told Joe and me to stay down, then guided us to the tree line into a waiting jeep.

We sped along a dirt road to a safe area out of range of the hail of bullets. Stopping at a small house, we took shelter inside. Our kindly escort told us a rival drug gang was trying to hijack our marijuana.

I imagined this was almost as bad as being shot down by the Viet Cong behind enemy lines, except in that instance, the Navy would not try to rescue us. In Jamaica, we would rot in prison or be killed by the rival gang.

The battle raged on for at least two hours with intermittent bursts of machinegun fire. We were falling behind schedule. The gunfire stopped. Our escort received a radio call that the landing strip was clear and the rival gang eliminated.

We headed back to the strip. To my relief, I found the plane unharmed, except the folding table in the back, which had been torn out. The leader of our supply gang asked me if I still wanted to take the load.

"I didn't survive a gun battle to return empty," I said.

He was happy and signaled to the crew to refuel the aircraft and load the bales of marijuana.

Joe and I, shaken but alive, were undeterred from completing our mission. My bravado would be a fatal decision. With the plane refueled and loaded, I fired up the engines, and we took off from the battle zone back to what we believed was the safety of North Carolina.

Immediately after landing in Wilmington, North Carolina, I got the first indication of trouble. It was night; we taxied to the fuel pumps and shut down. We were about to begin the refueling process when a gentleman wearing a police-style uniform approached the aircraft. I thought he was a law enforcement officer, and we were about to be arrested.

What I thought was a badge pinned to his left breast turned out to be a company logo. He was a rental car employee and wanted to know if we wanted to rent a car. Our relief was comforting but premature. Joe gave the fueler his credit card. We noticed he paid close attention to the underside of the aircraft.

I again fired up the engines, and we were off to Vermont. We later discovered the rental car employee had notified local law enforcement our aircraft had mud caked on the underbelly.

Shortly after takeoff, the FAA tried to contact us. I didn't answer. The only way of locating us was by 'skin paint' or track us on radar, which I was sure would not be the case. Local law enforcement must have contacted DEA with the aircraft's registration number and found it was home-ported in Burlington.

We later found out local police in North Carolina contacted the U.S. Customs Service in Wilmington, NC. They notified the Burlington DEA we had left the area, probably heading for Burlington International Airport.

We had a contingency plan to offload the marijuana at a vacant airfield near Burlington, but I proceeded directly to the Burlington Airport as planned, another fateful decision.

As we were entering Vermont airspace, I contacted the Burlington Tower for landing instructions. I could tell by the tower operator's voice something was not right. We landed and taxied to our hangar. I told Joe we needed to unload the airplane fast and get out of there.

The van was at the hangar, and no one else was around except my brother Paul. Paul, Joe, and I moved the drugs from the aircraft into the van in less than 2 minutes, and Paul departed the area.

Within seconds, two DEA agents dressed in raid jackets approached the airplane. The agents asked for permission to look inside, and I opened the door to empty aircraft. One agent, engaging me in some small talk while the other agent looked around the plane's interior, asked where we had been. I answered North Carolina,

I asked if Joe and I could push the aircraft into the hangar. The two DEA agents and a pair of local police officers helped us reposition the plane into the hangar, and I closed the overhead door.

As I felt a sense of calmness, thinking we might get away with this, the loud squelch of a two-way radio interrupted the still of the night. A loud voice came over the airwaves.

"We have a van loaded with pot, and the driver is under arrest."

Before I could take my next breath, Joe and I were in handcuffs. The once kindly DEA agent now pointing his weapon at me and reading our rights. Joe and I were patted down for weapons, escorted to a waiting vehicle, and placed into the backseat.

The agent in the passenger's seat taunted us. 'You guys are screwed.'

It was after midnight. Joe and I were so tired we could hardly keep our eyes open. Our careers as dope smugglers ended with a resounding thud almost as soon as it began.

After a brief ride, we pulled into some police barracks where we were fingerprinted, photographed, and interviewed in separate rooms. I knew my brother Paul and brother-in-law Joe well enough not to worry. They would not say a word to the agents.

I treated this as a capture by the Viet Cong. I was in enemy territory, in the hands of a more friendly foe. The agents and officers seemed content to have the three of us locked up and the dope off the street. After the booking and individual questioning, they placed us in separate cells. Much to our surprise, they never asked to give up the guys who hired us for this trip.

It was now 4:00 or 5:00 in the morning. I thought the DEA agents were as tired as we were and wanted to call it a day. The three of us agreed we would never testify against each other or Eddie Parker.

A few hours passed in our solitary cells. The jingle of keys and shouts of 'rise and shine folks, it's time to get ready for court' woke us to our new reality. It was a short ride to federal court. I was still in a daze. An attorney, dressed in a three-piece suit, sat with the three of us in a holding cell. He explained a man dressed in a tee shirt and jeans handed him a bag of money and gave instructions to get us out on bail and represent us as on this case.

The attorney met us at our initial hearing in front of the U.S. Magistrate, and we were released on bail. Joe, Paul, and I agreed with the statement of the agents the attorney read to us. We had been caught dead to rights smuggling drugs.

Joe and I just wanted to put this nightmare behind us and plead guilty. However, Paul was being stubborn and wanted to appeal the legality of the search.

While the motion to suppress the marijuana was in the appeals process., we all entered guilty pleas in federal court and throw ourselves at the mercy of the sentencing judge.

At sentencing, I explained to the judge I was the leader; it was my idea, and I convinced my two partners to join me in the venture. I was hoping the judge would give my two partners lesser sentences.

What I said was the plain truth, but it didn't matter. The judge was not moved—this was probably the biggest drug bust in Vermont history at the time—and my statement had no effect. We were sentenced to two years in federal prison and three years Special Parole. I was to report to the Federal Corrections Institution in Danbury, Connecticut, and begin serving my sentence in October 1983.

Jailhouse Rock

Facing the prospect of prison and financial ruin, Tony's options were limited. As a convicted felon with little opportunity, or time, to support his family, Tony faced a depressing low point in his life.

Where he once roamed the skies as a highly-skilled Naval aviator—hunting enemy pilots and reaching the pinnacle of his career by downing two enemy planes—he now faced a different life. He would be a chained eagle in federal prison surrounded by men who never had the opportunities he'd just tossed away. Surviving prison would be no less a challenge than dodging surface-to-air missiles and anti-aircraft guns.

In some ways, prison would be more of a challenge—he would face it alone. No wingman, no one to watch his back, no safe haven for his return. No one would come to his rescue.

Tony Nargi

It was now June, four months passed in a flash. I had broken the law and now faced the consequences. I didn't know how the system worked but knew at some point I could petition for parole. With credit for good behavior, I would be eligible after serving 14 months.

The summer of 1983 was depressing. I had no money and no prospect of accumulating any. I was facing at least a year and a half and maybe as much as five years in prison and was unemployable. My children were about to enter college, and I had no means of paying for it. I attempted to contact Parker to ask him for money, but he had vanished.

I was running out of time. My life was in a flat spin, and I had no ejection handle.

Once I reported to Danbury, it limited my options. I was desperate for money. The bank appraised the farm and house at $330,000. I paid for them in cash from savings and applied to a local bank for a mortgage. Still, the trauma of standing before a federal judge facing sentencing hadn't sunk in. I wasn't through taking risks that could destroy my life.

With some answers on the application, I lapsed into fiction. The bank would never grant me a mortgage if they knew of my circumstances. I ignored the first rule of hole digging; stop digging when you're at the bottom of a hole. Lying on an application to a federally insured bank is a felony.

I kept digging.

Based on my application, the bank approved a $160,000 mortgage—enough money to keep things going until I could find a long-term solution.

We lived in a small town in Vermont, so there was no doubt everyone knew of my arrest and conviction for drug smuggling. Strangely, no one said anything. I expected to be shunned, but that did not happen either. I worried about the effect on my wife and children. I'm sure they experienced something, but they never mentioned it.

Prison would contribute to worsening my situation, but I didn't know the terms of parole would make my situation even more depressing. But this was all in the murky, uncertain future. I was a decorated war veteran and a highly respected executive officer with a world-renowned defense contractor negotiating with the governments of Germany and Iran.

Now, I would be wearing an orange jumpsuit inside prison walls, just a number in a prison system where no one would care about my past achievements. They would just know me for what I was, a convicted drug smuggler.

October drew closer. I requested to change my reporting date to Danbury to after Christmas to spend the holidays with my family but was denied.

I had done everything I could to prepare myself for incarceration. Most of what I knew about prison I had learned from Hollywood. I was sure the Hollywood version was not an accurate depiction of prison life.

Turned out it was like the Navy. But I would find out what it was like when I got there, so I resolved to stop thinking about it. I had the unrealistic expectation someone would help me or make this nightmare disappear.

No one did.

There was no point in regret. The past is unalterable, the future uncertain. I would prepare as best I could. An old maxim of combat came to mind; 'No battle plan survives contact with the enemy.'

Face prison directly and adjust as necessary; that's what I would do. I tried not to let my thoughts affect my outward demeanor. It was important my family did not lose confidence in my ability to provide for them. This became a guiding principle of my behavior, keep up a brave front for my family.

I don't know how successful I was. I avoided contact with the outside world, but my wife could always see through me. No fooling her, try as I might. There was no return from my self-inflicted circumstances. Don't do the crime if you can't do the time now had a much more personal meaning.

How was I going to get back on track after release from federal prison? It seemed like an insurmountable problem. I would be a felon with no pilot's license, no security clearance, and on parole.

My wife drove with me from our home in Vermont to FCI Danbury in Danbury, Connecticut. The high barbed-wire walls with guards on patrol were intimidating. I took the keys from the ignition and handed them to my wife. She locked the doors, and we walked through the front door of the prison together.

Russ Protentis

Around the same time, another pilot from New England would face similar consequences. These two men—Tony Nargi and Dennis Pekarcik—would come to play an essential part in a significant case in my career. Tony would redeem himself somewhat for his past mistakes.

During the early 1980s, Dennis piloted charter flights on Cape Cod, the islands of Martha's Vineyard, and Nantucket. Craig Stewart, also a charter pilot, approached Dennis with a way to make a small fortune. Stewart said he wanted to smuggle marijuana from Colombia but did not have a co-pilot or the proper aircraft to complete the mission.

Stewart introduced Dennis to John Novak with a source of supply in Colombia. Novak needed pilots to operate an aircraft he owned to complete the journeys. Novak assured them of a safe landing with the drugs without facing inspection in Vermont because his friend was the airport manager in Rutland.

Dennis checked out Novak's Queen Air twin-engine aircraft and agreed to accompany Stewart on the trip. They would depart the airport in Rutland, Vermont, refuel in southern Georgia, and then proceed to northern Colombia. They would refuel and load 1200 pounds of marijuana on board. They would return to Georgia and refuel before heading back to Rutland, Vermont, after departing from Colombia.

The first trip went without a hitch. On the second journey, the results would be different.

After departing Colombia with a full load of marijuana,

they made a successful landing in Brunswick, Georgia to refuel. Then things took a turn for the worse. The shaded cabin windows and the odor of marijuana drew the unwanted attention of the airport maintenance crew.

In less than five minutes, officers of the Georgia Bureau of Investigations (GBI) surrounded the drug-laden aircraft.

Ironically, I was attending an advanced agent training seminar less than eight miles away at the Federal Law Enforcement Training Center in Glynco, Georgia. I spent six months there training as a Special Agent for the Bureau of Alcohol Tobacco and Firearms.

I would return to Glynco several times later in my career with United States Customs Service.

Because of the arrest in Georgia, Dennis, Craig Stewart, and John Novak, the mastermind of the operation, were convicted in U.S. District Court in Burlington, Vermont for importation and attempted distribution of marijuana. The trio was sentenced to federal prison.

Dennis would serve his time at FCI Danbury. In 1988, Dennis and Novak, who later cooperated with the U.S. Government, would re-establish their business relationship on a much larger scale.

And, in the fraternity-like environment of prison, Dennis would come to meet Tony Nargi and set them on a collision course with me in the not-too-distant future.

Washing the Money

In 1982, during the peak of the Colombian cocaine flood into the United States, President Ronald Reagan declared a renewed War on Drugs. The war started under President Richard Nixon. Reagan took it nuclear. The declaration would have a profound effect on the course of my career.

During my first two years as a Customs agent, I was assigned to a group investigating violations of the U.S. Arms Export Control Act. In 1984, Customs transferred me to a group specializing in money-laundering and narcotics smuggling.

My first money-laundering case, in January 1984, was investigating Massachusetts-based Rockland Trust Company. I was fortunate to work with one of the most diligent federal investigators I would ever meet in my career, IRS Special Agent Alfred 'Butch' DeAngelis. A tenacious investigator, DeAngelus would tirelessly sort through bank transaction records for ten hours a day.

Butch and I received information from the Financial Crimes Enforcement Network known as FinCen. FinCen is a financial analysis group made up of several federal agencies in the U.S. Treasury Department tasked with collecting and analyzing financial transactions to combat domestic and international money-laundering.

FinCen's review of deposits and withdrawals at the Rockland Trust revealed many transactions over $10,000.

In 1970, the United States established the Bank Secrecy Act to monitor suspicious transactions in banks. The legislation included a requirement for financial institutions to complete a Currency Transaction Report (CTR) when a customer withdrew or deposited more than $10,000 in cash in any one transaction.

The CTR, including the customer's social security number, was forwarded to the IRS. The CTR requirement targeted drug dealers depositing proceeds from their business in U.S. banks.

Rockland Trust Company failed to complete CTRs for several years, involving millions of dollars. The Assistant U.S. Attorney, Robert Mueller—who later rose to prominence as the head of the FBI among other accomplishments—believed we had enough information to prosecute Rockland Trust in Federal Court.

In September 1984, Mueller charged Rockland Trust Company in U.S. District Court in Boston with violations of the Bank Secrecy Act for failing to file Currency Transaction Reports with the IRS. Attorneys for the Company agreed to plead guilty to the indictment and paid a $50,000 fine.

Now experienced in investigating money-laundering cases, I expanded my role in the War on Drugs. As a U.S. Customs Special Agent on the war's front lines, I recruited cooperating witnesses who could aid my investigations.

My first potential recruits were two pilots from New England who had flown marijuana smuggling missions into the U.S. from Colombia and Jamaica. Released after serving federal prison time, they were now on probation or parole. Entering Tony Nargi and Dennis Pekarcik into the U.S. Customs database, I would get a notice and track their travels abroad.

After receiving one such alert from San Juan, Puerto Rico, I uncovered previous international arrivals into Miami, Florida, by both pilots. Further investigation located records of Nargi and Pekarcik arriving in the U.S. from Panama and the Dominican Republic. Their records and this travel from source countries sparked my interest.

I set up an appointment with Tom Weedock, New England Director of the U.S. Probation and Parole Department in Boston, MA. Based on the international travel violating their parole conditions, Nargi and Pekarcik faced revocation of their Special Federal Parole. They could serve up to six years in federal prison.

Instead of violating them, I asked Weedock to let me recruit the pilots as confidential sources. Mr. Weedock agreed; if they cooperated, he would approve my request to use them in an active undercover role.

Now it was up to me to recruit these two valuable assets to help our country in President Reagan's "War on Drugs."

As part of my efforts to recruit them, I dug into their arrest records. Both Dennis and Tony were arrested under similar circumstances—using similar methods—to smuggle the drugs. Both pilots served federal time in the Federal Correctional Facility in Danbury, Connecticut.

They were resourceful and soon devised a way to reduce their time served.

Tony proposed a ground aviation instruction course to the administration at Danbury; they would offer introductory instruction to fellow inmates interested in learning how to fly an airplane. They followed up on the teachings of two of FCI Danbury's most famous aviation aficionados, George Jung and Carlos Lehder.

Jung and Lehder were cellmates and alumni of Danbury FCI in the mid-1970s. After completing their sentence, they created Pablo Escobar's fleet of cocaine smuggling aircraft. At the peak of their post-graduate careers, Jung had a net worth of 100 million dollars and Lehder 2.7 billion dollars.

Their graduation from the 'University of FCI Danbury' led to very prosperous careers. Danbury, along with many of the U.S. Federal Prisons, had reputations as the stateside breeding grounds for operatives in both the Medellin and Cali cocaine cartels.

Lehder and Jung were operating outside the U.S., thus not in range of my targeting area.

However, Dennis lived in Yarmouth on Cape Cod, close to my home. Cape Cod was a well-known summer resort area in southeastern Massachusetts.

It was a sunny day in mid-May, a few weeks away from the start of summer vacation season on Cape Cod. This time of year, out-of-state residents and renters began their annual pilgrimage to the beach, which was an excellent time to approach Dennis.

My coworker, Special Agent Ken MacDonald, and I conducted surveillance of Dennis's home for three days. Yet no sign of him or his yellow 1969 Jaguar XJE. Our agency guidelines require two agents to be present when interviewing a witness or potential source. We had no idea if or when he might return and had other responsibilities.

McDonald would be away for a week traveling on another assignment. Unwilling to miss out on a great opportunity, I faced a dilemma, continue trying to find

Dennis by myself or wait for him to return. If I continued to look, I would violate agency policy by speaking to a source alone. Still, I was confident the results would outweigh the risk.

It was Friday around 11:00 AM, not a cloud in the sky and the aroma of the salty ocean permeating the air. The area was bustling with seasonal renters. My patience paid off. I finally laid eyes on Dennis driving a 1969 yellow Jaguar.

As he got out of the car, I pulled up beside the Jaguar. He stood 6'2", sporting a bronze Caribbean tan. Eyeing me with caution as I rolled down the window, I could see the concern on his face.

"Good morning, Dennis."

Visibly startled, he replied. "Do I know you?"

"Not really, but I know you quite well."

I showed him my badge and introduced myself. He somehow seemed relieved. He invited me into his home, and I sat at his kitchen table while he brewed us some tea. He said he expected somebody like me would visit him.

I explained to him the predicament he faced, violations of his parole and the possibility of going back to prison.

There was no hesitation; he would cooperate.

Despite the misconception about Club Fed being a comfortable place to do time, prison is never a pleasant experience. Going back was terrifying. It seemed the inevitability of someone like me catching up to him must have been weighing on him for years.

While at FCI Danbury, Dennis collected contact information of potential drug smuggling customers—something he could use to rebuild his lucrative smuggling business on release. All these inmates would trust him; prison builds bonds similar to those experienced in military service. With access to the wealth of information from those involved in major drug trafficking, a person with his background would prove invaluable.

I told him I would discuss the matter with his parole officer and be in touch.

The following Monday, I met with Tom Weedock. He gave me strict guidelines for using a federal parolee in an active investigation. There would be a monthly status report, signed by the Supervisory Agent in Charge of my office, detailing Dennis's cooperation, including any contact with known felons or narcotics traffickers. My boss, Christopher Nelson, the agent who would sign off on the report, agreed with this arrangement.

My next goal was to approach Tony. Tony differed from Dennis, presenting a different set of challenges. A graduate of the U.S. Naval Academy, and recipient of many medals and commendations for his heroics in the Vietnam War, Tony posed a more complicated situation. He might be less easy to intimidate by simple threats to his freedom.

Geography was also an obstacle.

Tony lived in Williston, Vermont, about three hours north of my office. I contacted Tony by telephone and said I wanted to meet him to discuss his federal parole violations. He was receptive and agreed to come to Boston the following day.

Tony arrived at the meeting thirty minutes early. He was a professional, and I approached him as such. After explaining his parole violation's ramifications, Tony seemed excited about the possibility of once again serving his country. Perhaps he saw this as a mea culpa for his past.

Good people make mistakes; here was a chance to make amends.

There were complications. Tony's parole officer in Vermont gave him permission to accept employment with a defense contractor selling small training airplanes to customers around the world. He asked if he could cooperate on a limited basis and work around his hectic schedule. Knowing his ability to infiltrate the drug smuggling underworld, I told him I would find the right fit for him. Once again, Tom Weedock approved using Tony in my investigations under the same conditions.

Now, it was time to put the two valuable assets to work.

After earning their release from FCI Danbury, Tony and Dennis, who had become friends inside, remained in contact. Tony used his experience to set up a commercial charter aircraft company operating flights between Florida, Central America, and the Caribbean. By targeting potential customers in Florida, it would allow them to fly for a living.

Avoiding violations of their federal parole created a problem. These conditions—designed to reduce re-offending—hampered the business plan. They had to avoid contact with other felons. In the charter airline business, it would be almost impossible. Drug trafficking was a huge market, and smugglers paid cash—something every business could use to minimize taxable income and grow their client base.

Any travel outside of their state of residence required prior approval of the Director of Probation and Parole in Boston, MA. Travel outside the U.S. would raise suspicions.

Tony, living in Florida flying airplanes, was one continuous parole violation. He'd call-forwarded his Vermont phone number, so calls from his parole officer would appear to reach him in there instead of Florida.

Tony added to his already extensive parole violations

when he worked with Dennis. Now they were both parole violators involved in a business that lent itself to drug smuggling. While their time at FCI Danbury brought these two experienced pilots together, it did not afford them the same level of connections as Jung and Lehder.

Jung and Lehder developed a fleet of pilots with no criminal convictions in the U.S. They connected to sources in South America and could use them to their advantage. They could use others to take the risk of flying the planes, shielding their involvement.

In their circumstances, Tony and Dennis took the risk, and they needed to build a business with new customers.

Miami, Florida, the U.S. hub for drug smugglers, became the home base for Tony's business. An attorney in Miami leased an aircraft for the business venture. The Cheyenne Piper 42, a turboprop executive long-range aircraft, was ideal for transporting business clients at home and abroad.

The attorney also introduced Tony to Armando Fiallo, a fluent English-speaking businessman from Panama. Fiallo hired Tony for frequent flights from Miami to Panama City, Panama. While never overtly about smuggling, these flights followed a telling pattern; the men always carried one small bag and one large, heavy suitcase.

The destination in Panama, a safe haven for banks that held large cash deposits for narcotics smugglers from the U.S., was more evidence of the most likely scenario.

Fiallo's associates would take one-way trips in the Cheyenne from Miami to Panama City, Panama. Once passengers left with their baggage, Tony would refuel and fly the empty aircraft back to Miami. The pattern never changed, and Tony was more than willing to practice willful ignorance of his passengers' activity.

After four or five successful trips, Fiallo introduced Tony to Bernard Yip. Yip was a Dominican-born Asian who had become a U.S. citizen and owned several casinos in the Dominican Republic (D.R.). He needed a plane and pilots to transport him from the D.R. to Miami and other destinations.

Tony agreed to work with Yip on a weekly retainer. What Tony didn't know, or chose not to, was the Yip family operated one of the most extensive cocaine smuggling operations in the Caribbean. Dennis, recently released from prison, traveled to Miami, Florida, and reconnected with Tony. Bernard Yip met Dennis and hired him to be Tony's co-pilot.

The biggest problem facing narcotics smugglers is cleaning the money from their narcotics sales. On one of his money-laundering trips, Yip hired the pilots to fly him and his wife from Miami to Santo Domingo.

Yip and his wife arrived at Miami International private aviation area and met Tony and Dennis at the plane. Yip introduced his wife Maria, who was very pleasant to behold. She wore a tight skirt above the knees and had long flowing black hair, dark brown eyes and high cheekbones, and a dark tanned olive complexion.

Yip told the pilots to load Maria's suitcases and his two large duffle bags onto the aircraft. The two raced to Maria's side. The duffle bags were heavy, easily weighing over one hundred pounds each. The pilots knew not to ask questions; they were happy to have an income. Charting a flight from Miami to Santo Domingo, D.R., they took off with the attractive woman, her husband, and the heavy luggage likely full of drug money.

The flight was uneventful, and a few hours later, they landed in Santo Domingo. During the flight, Maria told the pilots she had won several beauty contests in the Caribbean. She had many beautiful girlfriends in Santo Domingo who would love to meet two American pilots. It added more interest to the journey for two very naïve pilots.

At Las Americas International Airport in Santo Domingo, Tony and Dennis offered to off-load the four bags from the aircraft for Dominican Customs Inspection. Yip said he and his wife would take the two small suitcases and told Tony and Dennis to stay with the plane to refuel it. The two large duffle bags would remain onboard while he took care of the Customs Inspectors.

By the greeting Yip received from the inspectors, it was evident he had done this before. Dominican Customs would review the pilots' passports, Yip told them, but would not search the aircraft. Returning a short time later without his wife, Yip asked the pilots to chart a flight to San Juan, Puerto Rico, as he had some business to attend.

Tony charted a course to San Juan without thinking about the ramifications, and off they went. It would be a mistake putting Tony and Dennis in the crosshairs of the United States Customs Service and my investigation.

Tony Nargi

Yip told us we would be meeting some of his associates when we landed in San Juan. While making our approach to Luis Munoz Marin International Airport, Yip said the aircraft would be clearing U.S. Customs in San Juan. He would do all the talking to the Customs Inspector in the private aviation area.

As we taxied to the terminal, Yip reminded us to follow his lead and to remember he was 'the Boss.' He made it clear we should follow his orders.

After shutting down the engines, Yip had us grab the large duffle bags and wheel them into the terminal. It was a sweltering and humid day. The duffle bags felt heavier, although they never left the plane in Santo Domingo. Walking into the U.S. Customs and Immigration Hall, Yip was confident and self-assured. Dennis and I were less so.

Although I wasn't certain about what was in the bags, I was sure it wasn't strictly legal.

Dressed in an expensive tailored suit, smiling and cordial, Yip seemed to know everyone there. He held a large box of candy in his left hand as he approached the counter where a rather large female Customs Inspector named Yolanda sipped on a fruit drink.

Yolanda greeted Yip with a smile.

"Welcome back. Mr. Yip," she said, as he presented her a box of imported chocolates. 'You always remember me,' she added, as they exchanged pleasantries.

"I am again declaring money from my casino in

Santo Domingo, and my pilots have the bags with them."

"How much this time?"

"Three million. We are doing well; you are welcome to visit as our guest any time."

Yolanda seemed unfazed, like someone declaring they had three million dollars with them was an everyday thing. It was apparent this was not an uncommon occurrence with Yip. She handed him a Customs Declaration Form, then gave Dennis and me declaration forms to complete and returned to her.

After completing the form, Yip asked if Yolanda wanted to count the money.

"We haven't the last three times, so why would we start now?" They had a good laugh together. Yolanda turned more serious. "These pilot's faces are new to me, so I need to see their passports."

We complied, but my heart raced. While thumbing through the pages of our passports, Yolanda typed something into the computer. She reviewed the documents, including the Customs declaration and currency transaction forms, then returned them.

I relaxed once she'd handed back my passports.

Yip asked Yolanda if she finished the paperwork.

She smiled and said, "Enjoy Miami."

We breathed a sigh of relief and dragged the bags into a waiting limousine outside the terminal. Yip said we'd done a great job and handed us each a one thousand dollars bonus.

I was just happy to be past the Customs checkpoint without getting arrested.

Russ Protentis

Tony and Dennis made two similar trips for the Yips in the following weeks. Their business thrived on the largesse of the new drug customers—it would not last long.

By completing the Customs Declaration Form 6059, the pilots confirmed their arrival on an international flight—creating problems for themselves. As federal parolees, they were prohibited from traveling internationally and from being together. The document, confirming they had violated two conditions of their federal parole, put them in my crosshairs.

It would be this self-inflicted wound that left them little choice but to cooperate with me.

After reviewing the list of potential targets from Tony

and Dennis, I focused on Dennis's former cellmate, Johnny. Johnny Villa was at FCI Danbury for his part in an organized crime narcotics distribution ring.

Johnny told Dennis the organization needed a pilot to transport marijuana and cocaine from Jamaica into Boston. He was one of the many drug contacts Dennis made in prison. This organized crime group seemed like the best target to pursue. Meanwhile, Tony detailed his association with several money-laundering organizations in Florida.

Armando Fiallo and Bernard Yip, two of Tony's clients, were both targets of money-laundering investigations by the U.S. Department of Justice in Washington DC. I forwarded information on Yip and Fiallo to the U.S. Customs Service Office of Investigations in San Juan, Puerto Rico.

Special Agent Ben Garcia, assigned to the San Juan office, would travel to Boston to interview Tony. He asked me to arrange the interview. Accompanied by Assistant United States Attorney Joanne Masurek, Garcia met me in Boston and laid out their information.

Masurek told me Fiallo, a Panamanian national, had a close association with Panamanian General Manuel Noriega. She wanted to know if Tony met with Noriega during his trips to Panama.

Tony said he met no one in Panama but recounted his

relationship with Fiallo and his associates. Masurek and Garcia interviewed Dennis and Tony together regarding their trips for Bernard Yip.

Tony and Dennis laid out the standard pattern for these trips. Each ending with the delivery of millions in cash to a bank in Puerto Rico.

After the interviews, Tony and Dennis left for their hotels; I remained behind to discuss the investigation with Masurek and Garcia.

Garcia said Yip made similar trips with another pilot in a smaller plane. Masurek said sources familiar with Yip, including his former pilot, confirmed the transport of large amounts of money.

Yip owned several casinos in the Dominican Republic and was importing hundreds of kilos of cocaine into the U.S. He couldn't deposit these large amounts of money in U.S. banks without alerting the IRS. Yip devised a scheme to hide his drug proceeds within his profit from casinos. Masurek told me one source in the Dominican Republic had copies of accounting records for Yip's casino. The profits fell far below the sums of the cash he was declaring to U.S. Customs in San Juan.

Masurek said on a recent trip to San Juan from Santo Domingo, Yip declared he was importing $3 million. This was the money in the two duffle bags Tony and Dennis dragged into Customs. However, a source in Miami who helped him pack the suitcases said the suitcases contained $1.5 million in casino profits. Garcia said this would allow Yip to deposit $1.5 million from casino revenues and $1.5 million from drug proceeds into a U.S. bank without raising suspicions.

Yip purchased real estate in Florida to further conceal his profits from drug distribution. Masurek and Garcia said they would use Tony's and Dennis's statements in civil forfeiture proceedings by the Department of Justice to seize Yip's bank accounts in the U.S.

The next day, I drove Masurek, Garcia, and Tony to the airport to catch their flights home. Dennis would head home to Yarmouth, MA. We would get together the following morning to plan a meeting with Johnny and begin phase two.

Goodfellas

On the drive to Dennis's place in Yarmouth, Massachusetts, I would pass by a Burger King off the main Highway. In the parking lot of Burger King was a bank of six public telephones. Before the widespread acceptance of cell phones—or the adaptation of pay-as-you-go "burner" phones—public telephones were the preferred form of communication between narcotics smugglers and traffickers. Avoiding monitoring by law enforcement wiretaps and intercepts made for intelligent business practice.

Most traffickers carried rolls of quarters in their pockets for placing calls to their associates. It was something smart cops would notice. While not in and of themselves incriminating, a pocketful of quarters might be a good indication of a drug dealer.

Public telephones were more difficult for law enforcement to monitor. They allowed criminals to discuss business openly without fear of investigators gathering incriminating evidence. Drug smugglers and distributors rarely discussed their business on home or office telephones.

Armed with a handful of quarters, Dennis called Johnny,

who was pleased to hear his voice. Dennis said he was looking for work. Johnny said he had plenty. They met the following day at 10:00 AM, at the First Stop Donut Shop in the Chelsea Produce Market north of Boston.

The New England Mob controlled the market, making it difficult for law enforcement to operate without detection. To watch this place, we'd have to be cautious.

Outfitting Dennis with a transmitter disguised as a digital pager for me to listen and record his conversation, we sent him inside the donut shop. I found an excellent surveillance spot between two construction trailers facing the shop. It would be almost impossible for anyone to spot me from the market area.

Around 10:00 A.M., a brown two-door Cadillac Coupe Deville parked next to Dennis's Jaguar. A tall and slender man, matching Johnny's prison photograph, and another heavyset man got out of the car, greeting Dennis in the entryway of the donut shop. The man with Johnny probably weighed well over 300 pounds. He introduced himself as Tony.

Although I was nearly half a mile away from the donut shop, I heard the conversation as clear as if I were in the entryway with them.

Tony said he worked for some serious people, and one

of them would like to meet Dennis. He would call "the guy" who was in the produce market looking for any surveillance. These guys made it clear they would keep Dennis very busy but warned him there'd be severe consequences if he screwed with them. Dennis said he understood the risk.

While the conversation was on, I noticed a maroon-colored Lincoln Town Car park next to Tony's Cadillac. A silver-haired man, probably in his fifties, got out of the Lincoln then went inside the donut shop, taking a seat next to Johnny. He introduced himself as Murray.

I drove by the restaurant to grab the license plates from the Cadillac and the Lincoln. The vanity plate on the Lincoln read MARINO.

Tony told Murray that Dennis was a pilot with experience flying planes to Colombia. He could be trusted because he did time with Johnny at FCI Danbury. Murray said this was probably the only time they would meet; Tony would handle the rest of the arrangements.

Murray said he wanted Dennis to find an aircraft capable of transporting one ton of marijuana per week from Jamaica to Boston. They would pay $100,000 per trip. After a couple of successful trips with the marijuana, they would send Dennis back to Colombia to transport 500 kilos of cocaine a week from Colombia to Boston.

Dennis said he needed cash to find an aircraft capable of making these trips. Murray told him there was plenty of funding available and that he should deal with Tony about all the arrangements. The meeting ended, and Tony provided Dennis with his telephone number and instructed him to call the following week from a public telephone.

Now I had to do my homework and compile all the background data I could find on Murray and Tony. Tony's Cadillac Coupe Deville, registered to an Anthony Rizzo of Revere, Massachusetts. His driver's license photo was a perfect match for "Tony." Murray's vehicle was registered to Marino Sarno, also of Revere. His driver's license photo was also a match.

A criminal record check showed Rizzo was convicted in Boston Superior Court for illegal possession of a firearm. Sarno, along with fourteen other defendants, had been indicted by a Federal grand jury for possession with intent to distribute 50,000 lbs. of marijuana found on board a fishing vessel in Rockland, Maine.

I contacted my friend Ed Walsh, the Deputy Superintendent of the Boston Police Department Intelligence Division, about Rizzo and Sarno and their potential connections to organized crime. I had worked with Walsh in 1985 while assigned to the U.S. Customs Service

Regional Intelligence Unit.

Walsh said we would meet his cousin, FBI Special Agent John Connolly. According to Walsh, Connolly was the foremost expert on New England organized crime.

The following day, Walsh and I met with Connolly. He jumped in my car and directed us toward the North End of Boston.

Connolly was a wealth of information.

Anthony Rizzo was a made member of La Cosa Nostra in Boston. He rose to this status, considered a high honor within the mob, after taking the fall on a weapons charge for William Ierardi.

Ierardi, a known cocaine distributor for the Boston mob, was a passenger in Rizzo's car pulled over by Boston Police in the city's Charlestown section. Rizzo claimed the firearm under the passenger's seat, where Ierardi was sitting, was his own, not Ierardi's. His loyalty earned him his "bones" within the mob.

No stranger to law enforcement, Ierardi had been implicated in the gangland-style massacre at the infamous Blackfriars Restaurant on June 28, 1978.

The Blackfriars Massacre, named for the location of the incident, The Blackfriars bar, was a vicious murder of five men. Police suspected it was an attempted robbery of a drug-dealer gone bad. The victims, discovered dead on the floor in a cramped basement office by the janitor opening the pub in the morning, suffered multiple gunshot wounds.

They were a notorious group of mob associates and one former investigative reporter who liked to associate with them.

Vincent Solmonte, age 35, owner of the Blackfriars Pub.

Peter Meroth, age 31, of the Jamaica Plain neighborhood of Boston.

Freddy Delavega, 34, of Somerville.

Charles Magarian, 37, of North Andover.

John "Jack" Kelly, 34, a journalist who worked as a night manager of the pub, was once employed as an investigative reporter for WBZ news radio and WNAC-TV.

The suspects were an equally nefarious group;

James J. "Whitey" Bulger, of Somerville, Massachusetts, leader of the Winter Hill Gang, an Irish- American crime family in Boston. Bulger was an informant for John Connolly of the FBI.

Stephen "The Rifleman" Flemmi, of Roxbury, Massachusetts, a former member of the Winter Hill Gang, also an informant for the FBI.

Nicholas Femia, of East Boston, Massachusetts, an associate of the Patriarca crime family and the Winter Hill

Gang involved in extortion and armed robbery.

James Martorano, contract killer, member of the Winter Hill Gang and the Patriarca crime family, a close friend of Kelly.

While police suspected the involvement of the above men, they charged only two men with the murders. Robert Italiano of East Boston, Massachusetts and William N. Ierardi, a drug dealer from Lynn, Massachusetts, were tried and found not guilty after trial in 1979.

This high-profile case remains unsolved.

These guys were serious players; we would have to be careful. If they even had a hint Dennis was cooperating, they'd kill him.

According to Connolly, Rizzo, also known as 'Fats,' was an enforcer for the New England La Cosa Nostra. He collected payments for narcotics and bookmaking. Rizzo lived on North Margin Street in Boston's North End, less than a city block from the Boston Mob Headquarters at 98 Prince Street.

Connolly, often interrupted by his digital pager's alert tone, requested they drop him off after each page at Joe Tecce's Restaurant, a famous dining establishment in the North End of Boston. Walsh told me that Connolly would receive a call from "his source" on a public telephone phone in that location's lower level.

Years later, I discovered the source calling Connolly on the public telephone phone was James Whitey Bulger, the famed Boston Irish Mafia head. Connolly gained Bulger's cooperation, a neighborhood friend, as part of his effort to dismantle the Italian-dominated New England organized crime family. Bulger's cooperation with Connolly was initially viewed as a rousing success.

However, during the investigation, Connolly became involved in Bulger's Criminal Enterprise and is now serving a life sentence in Florida for his part in a murder ordered by Bulger.[1]

A long-term federal grand jury investigation conducted by Department of Justice Assistant U.S. Attorney John Durham revealed Connolly tipped off Bulger about an impending arrest warrant for him and his associate, Stephen "The Rifleman" Flemmi.

Durham, who I met when he interviewed me about my relationship with Connolly, impressed me as a relentless prosecutor who left no investigative lead unturned. He later worked for former Attorney General William Barr as the lead

---

[1] Connolly, diagnosed with terminal cancer, was recently granted compassionate release from prison.

investigator reviewing the Mueller Report on President Trump.

I now had all the ingredients for a narcotics investigation worthy of federal prosecution, with some additional steps. The problem being I was working for an agency permeated with politics. The U.S. Customs Office of Investigations in Boston had never attempted a proactive investigation.

Narcotics investigations conducted by the Boston office were basically a response to smuggled narcotics seized by the Coast Guard, Customs Inspectors at the airport, or the result of International DEA investigations. Customs agents would arrest smugglers detained by their own inspection service or another agency, secure the drugs, and wait to turn the evidence and prisoners over to the DEA for prosecution.

My supervisor, Jim Burke, told me I would conduct this investigation under the supervision of DEA. U.S. Customs had never seen a case developed like this one, and they would rely on the DEA and FBI to direct any future steps.

Burke said he would contact the local DEA field office and coordinate this investigation with the FBI and/or DEA.

Burke arranged a meeting for me with DEA Group Supervisor Jim Forget. Forget said that the case I presented was "small potatoes" and that a ton of marijuana falls off the back of a truck every day.

One of the DEA agents in the meeting with Forget, Gary O'Hara, stopped me in the hallway as I left the office. He said the case had excellent potential and would be glad to work with me on it. O'Hara and I began our joint investigation. Neither O'Hara nor I felt comfortable with FBI agent Connolly. We deliberately kept him out of the loop, and as it turned out, for good reason.

O'Hara and I took a ride to Cape Cod. We met with Dennis, listening in as he returned a telephone call to Rizzo where they arranged to meet in Chelsea at the 1st Stop Donut Shop.

The following day, Dennis arrived at the donut shop, greeted in the entryway by Johnny and Anthony. Anthony told Dennis to drive down North Margin Street in the North End of Boston in one hour, beep the horn, and he would have a package for him. Anthony told Dennis he would receive a bag containing enough money to travel and locate an aircraft big enough to smuggle at least one ton of marijuana from Jamaica into Boston.

Dennis agreed, left the donut shop, and went to a public telephone bank where he paged me to contact him.

I told Dennis to follow through with Rizzo's instructions and meet with us at the 99 Restaurant in Charlestown after receiving the money.

It was a beautiful sunny summer day in June, and we watched as Dennis drove his Jaguar convertible slowly down North Margin Street. He honked the horn, and Rizzo, leaning out a window on the third floor at 62 North Margin, dropped a paper bag directly into the passenger's seat of the Jaguar.

It was like pennies from heaven, a lot of pennies.

Dennis waved, then drove to the 99 Restaurant, where I retrieved the paper bag containing thirty crisp new $100 bills wrapped in a rubber band. I counted the money, $3,000, and logged it into evidence. We paid Dennis $750.00 for his expenses on the case to date.

Within a few days, Rizzo contacted Dennis from a public telephone.

"Get ahold of your friend Tony and line up a plane. We have a trip down south."

"It'll cost 15 to 20k to lease the plane, " Dennis said.

"No problem. Just get Tony. and we'll meet," Rizzo said,

Tony was in Vermont, so I arranged for him to be available for this meeting.

The following week, Rizzo and Sarno met with Dennis and Tony in the Chelsea produce market at the donut shop. Sarno had photographs and coordinates of a landing strip in Jamaica. The plan called for the pilots to load 1000-2000 lbs.

of marijuana on their aircraft, then fly it to an airport of their choice in the United States.

Tony said he was familiar with many of the landing strips in Jamaica. The one Rizzo and Sarno chose for this operation was too short and would not be suitable for an aircraft loaded with 1000-2000 pounds of cargo on board.

Rizzo and Sarno were disappointed but said they would contact their guy in Jamaica and find another landing site. After the meeting with Sarno and Rizzo, I met with Dennis and Tony to discuss targeting this group.

Tony said the crew was very disorganized. It would be months before they ever found a suitable runway to complete this operation. We put the investigation of these "Goodfellas" on the backburner.

Russ Protentis (red shirt/center) and other agents

with significant cocaine seizure

Lt. Tony Nargi's F-8 C on the Aircraft Carrier

Intrepid

Russ Protentis and the Attorney General of the

United States Alberto Gonzales

Russ Protentis in front of Air Force One

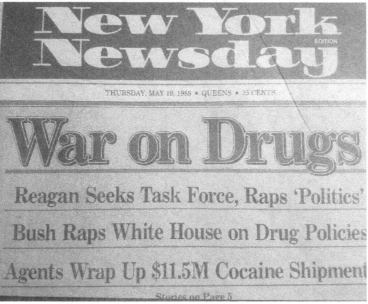

The plane that was seized in Miami.

The Fugitive

After the case against Rizzo and Sarno went on the backburner, Dennis told us about a call from a mutual friend, someone who had served time with him at Danbury FCI, named John Novak. Novak wanted to know if Dennis was still in touch with Tony and if they were still looking for some work.

Dennis said he would let him know.

"Now is as good a time as any to return the call," I said.

We found a payphone, and Dennis hit up Novak on his pager. While we waited, I hooked up a tape recorder to the phone.

U.S. Customs Service guidelines authorized one-party consent to a recording with the approval of a U.S. Attorney. This included telephone or in-person meetings with targets of an investigation, preserving the tapes for evidence in future court trials.

Within ten minutes, the phone rang. Novak and Dennis used cautious words to talk about good old times for a few minutes, then Novak delved into his proposal.

"Me and some friends from college (FCI Danbury) are gonna lease a car," Novak said. "Tony will know how to drive (meaning a plane). We want him to go down south (fly to Colombia) and then head home (New York.)

"Would he be driving any passengers (cargo)?" Dennis asked.

"Yeah, at least a thousand pairs of very expensive sneakers (kilos of cocaine)."

"How much to do the driving?

"You split a commission, 3-4 dollars a pair (three to four thousand dollars per kilo of cocaine) for each trip."

Novak wanted Dennis to come to New York to talk in person. He would send a prepaid ticket and wire one thousand dollars by Western Union for travel expenses. He was eager to arrange the trip.

"We can talk when you get up here, but we want to make the pickup within the next two to three months."

My office had little if any expertise in dealing with informants in narcotics smuggling investigations, especially proactively.

Upper-level management in the Boston office made many trips to Miami, the Caribbean, and other exotic locales purportedly to learn the ins-and-outs of narcotics smuggling trends and investigations.

However, I learned the attendees spent a lot of time brushing up on their golf game, and they never missed a happy hour. Managing proactive investigations was not a top priority, except as window dressing by these junkets.

One result of this inexperience led to the death of John McIntyre, a prized informant. Ineptitude and incompetence tipped off notorious gangster, FBI informant, and future member of the FBI's Most-Wanted List, James "Whitey" Bulger, to McIntyre's cooperation.

McIntyre worked on many of Bulger's arms and narcotics smuggling operations as a boat hand and captain on several ocean-going vessels, including the Valhalla. In 1984, the Valhalla transferred weapons brought from the United States to an Irish Republican Army (IRA) controlled ship, the Marita Ann, off Ireland's coast.

In November 1984, McIntyre guided the Ramsland, a Norwegian freighter laden with thirty-six tons of marijuana, into Boston Harbor. U.S. Customs seized the boat.

Despite information from the FBI that Bulger believed McIntyre was one of only two individuals who could have "given up the Valhalla and the Ramsland," my office authorized $20,000 in "front money."

The ill-conceived plan called for McIntyre to deliver the money to Pat Nee—a notorious bank robber and associate of the IRA — with hopes Bulger's crew would allow him to invest in the next big load of marijuana destined for Boston.

At a South Boston restaurant, the Irish enclave of the city, McIntyre met with Nee. The $20,000 payment from McIntyre, who didn't have two nickels to rub together, confirmed he was a rat in Bulger's mind.

McIntyre was never seen alive again.

Torturing him before killing him as punishment for his betrayal—Bulger removed McIntyre's teeth and fingernails—they buried him under the basement of a home at 799 Third Street, South Boston. The house was owned by Pat Nee's brother, Michael.

McIntyre became another Irish casualty of the Troubles and Bulger's terror campaign in Boston, protected by the FBI.

Bulger's crew later dug up McIntyre's remains from the basement, then reburied them, absent the missing teeth, in a shallow gravesite down a slope from the Southeast Expressway and across the street from the Florian Hall in Dorchester, Massachusetts.

If Irish symbolism was the goal or just a convenient spot to get rid of a body, we'll never know, but the remains didn't stay undiscovered for long. On a frigid night in near zero-degree weather, Massachusetts State Police Investigators excavated the remains of McIntyre's bones.

I knew enough about my case—and the potential my

informants offered—not to make any such mistakes and lose these assets. I also knew, to succeed, we had to be proactive. Stemming the flow of drugs would fail by just reacting to chance arrests of the odd smuggler coming into U.S. ports of entry. It would require a novel approach to investigations beyond anything done by Customs before.

The Customs Service hierarchy told me my informants could not fly into Colombia or any other foreign locations as part of an investigation of narcotics smuggling. I argued that DEA agents/pilots and informants regularly flew into Colombia and several Caribbean Islands as part of undercover investigations.

My bosses—Jim Burke, Haig Sohegian, the Regional Commissioner for U.S. Customs Enforcement, and William Simmons, the Acting SAC for the Boston Field Office of Investigations—summonsed me to a meeting. They said I had lost my mind and directed me to inform the U.S. Customs SAC in New York. We were not running this investigation. It was not our area of expertise.

As a minor concession, Sohegian said I could stay with the case to gather intelligence.

Undeterred, in early 1988, I sought an alternative plan. I called John Murray, an agency friend and retired New York City Police Officer. The U.S. Customs Service hired Murray as a technical surveillance support officer for the SAC in New York.

In 1987, John invited me to attend the Air Smuggling Investigators Association (Asia) conference in New York City. We had Tony Nargi speak—under an alias and from behind a curtain—on current air smuggling techniques. The segment Tony Nargi taught was the highlight of the conference.

Murray had a stellar reputation in the New York Office. He had been assisting me on telephone intercepts of Anthony Rizzo. I explained the obstacles I was facing in the investigation. He suggested I contact his good friend Mike Nestor, Resident Agent in Charge (RAIC) for the U.S. Customs Office of Investigation in the city of Bohemia on Long Island.

Murray connected me to Nestor. Once I explained the case, Nestor said I should contact David McAndrew, a Group Supervisor in his office. McAndrew, who had also transferred to the U.S. Customs Service from ATF, seemed interested.

McAndrew wanted Dennis and I to travel to New York and meet with him soon. He expressed shock the Boston office didn't want to pursue this matter and would give it up to another office. Usually, assets and cases like this are jealously guarded by the office initiating the case.

I met with Dennis and had him contact Nova. Dennis told him he would be in New York in the next few days. During the recorded conversation, Novak said he would wire $1,000 to Dennis by Western Union in the next hour.

As promised, one hour later, there was $1,000 waiting for Dennis at Western Union in Hyannis. Novak was interested in moving things along. The following day, Dennis and I were on our way to New York to meet McAndrew and Bob Carbonari, a Special Agent assigned to his group.

At LaGuardia Airport, Dennis and I met McAndrew and Carbonari at the U.S. Customs Service Office. I played recordings of the telephone conversation between Dennis and Novak. Dennis said Novak went by the name John Joyce because he was a fugitive from justice.

Carbonari confirmed Novak's fugitive status. He had fled prosecution for conspiring to smuggle marijuana and hashish into California on behalf of Mexico's infamous Sinaloa Cartel. Novak also conspired to import several tons of Thai sticks—high-quality marijuana wrapped in leaves—into California.

McAndrew, Carbonari, and I agreed we would keep Novak's fugitive status under wraps for the time being. If the U.S. Attorney's Office became aware, they likely would order us to arrest him. It would derail this undercover smuggling investigation before we ever got started.

We had Dennis call Novak to arrange a meeting. Novak was elated Dennis was in New York. He asked him to take a taxi to the Carlyle Hotel at East 76th Street and Madison Ave in the Upper East Side of Manhattan.

"When you get here," Novak said, "I'll jump in, and we can ride to my apartment."

Dennis flagged down a cab and headed off to the Carlyle with Carbonari and I following right behind.

At the hotel, Novak got in the cab. We followed them to a high-rise apartment building at 515 East 72nd Street. Dennis and Novak left the cab and headed inside.

It would be the last we would see or hear of Dennis for the next twenty-four hours.

We had decided not to wire him up, fearing it being discovered by Novak. While Novak called Dennis first, drug dealers—especially ones with past arrest problems or wanted fugitives—were a paranoid bunch. We had no idea who else might show up and search Dennis for a wire.

For the time being, he was on his own.

We also chose not to run any surveillances. Too risky without knowing all the players.

As the following day came around, we'd heard nothing

from Dennis. We second-guessed ourselves.

Had Novak taken Dennis to Colombia, where a plane loaded with cocaine was waiting for him to fly to the U.S.? Or worse, was he undergoing intense interrogation by members of the Medellin Cocaine Cartel in Colombia?

At 2:00 pm, I got an alert on my pager to contact a phone number in the 212-area code. I called the number, a public telephone, and was elated to hear Dennis's voice on the other end.

"I'm back in the lobby of the Carlyle Hotel," he said. "What do you want me to do now?"

We had to find a place to meet, taking precautions to ensure Novak, or some unknown associate, wasn't following Dennis, and we had to move fast.

Carbonari and I were in the waiting room at Sloan-Kettering Cancer Treatment Center with McAndrew while visiting his father. McAndrew suggested we meet here. It was close to the Carlyle with lots of people around.

"Come to Sloan-Kettering," I said. "Ask for McAndrew's room and go to the waiting area on that floor."

The three of us waited anxiously for Dennis's arrival. Fifteen minutes later, he walked in.

There were four for five other people in the waiting room, including two patients, who would soon witness a scene out of a movie.

Dennis told us the details of his overnight meeting with Novak. As we feared, Novak was not alone. Robert Krevsky was waiting in the apartment when Dennis and Novak arrived.

Novak was expecting Dennis to return in twenty minutes. He'd told Dennis to contact his friends from a public telephone, hoping he could help locate an airplane. Krevsky and Dennis knew each other from years ago when they'd stolen an Aero Commander Turbo twin-engine plane from the Municipal Airport in Beverly, MA. The plan was to steal the aircraft and travel to Colombia to pick up 300 kilograms of cocaine.

The plan, involving Dennis, Krevsky, and a third man, failed when the plane became low on fuel, forcing them to land at Fort Lauderdale International Airport. The airport was closed for refueling. Fearing detection by law enforcement, the trio abandoned the stolen plane and fled.

As to the latest plan, Novak gave Dennis an envelope containing $10,000 in 100-dollar bills. Dennis took the envelope out of his jacket pocket and handed it to us. We confirmed the amount, raising the eyebrows in the room even higher.

"Novak said he had a couple of keys (kilos) of cocaine on

hand," Dennis said. "And he showed me a duffle bag full of cash. Must have been at least two hundred grand."

Novak and Krevsky, working together, had been "moving" 20 to 30 kilos of cocaine a month for the past year. Krevsky said his "coke" supplier was a close associate of Pablo Escobar. Escobar was looking for some planes and pilots to transport cocaine by air from Colombia to New York City.

"He wants me to locate a plane that could fly non-stop from northern Colombia to New York or New Jersey," Dennis said. "Krevsky said the Colombians were losing far too many loads of cocaine while their airplanes were refueling in the southern U.S. or Caribbean Islands.

"Novak knew about me getting popped in Brunswick, Georgia while refueling the plane with a load of grass. Krevsky's supplier, named Gus, said the Medellin Cocaine Cartel wanted to move their cocaine trafficking route to New York.

"Escobar's people wanted the planes to make four or five trips each month, and he would pay me $3,000 to $4,000 for each kilo of coke that arrived in the U.S.."

Dennis told us how Novak and Krevsky spent the remainder of the evening and following day discussing potential routes Dennis should take while traveling from

Colombia to New York.

Krevsky had to leave several times to pick up money and would always return with food. Dennis told them he would work on getting an airplane. Novak gave him the envelope and told him to find something quickly. The three men did a few lines of coke, then Dennis left to "go find a plane."

Instead, he came to meet with us at Sloan-Kettering.

A criminal record check on Krevsky showed an arrest in Iowa in 1983 for attempting to lease an aircraft to transport cocaine from Colombia into the United States from an undercover FBI agent.

Now we knew these guys were serious.

While in the waiting room at the Cancer Center, which we turned into a makeshift command center, I reached out to contacts who ran an undercover operation offering lease aircraft and boats to entice drug smugglers to use their services.

The U.S. Customs Service Office in Mobile, Alabama, ran Operation Skymaster. I spoke with Special Agent Ernie Winberg and his partner Special Agent Ernst "Jake" Jacobsen. The two southern gentlemen were very kind and professional, ready and willing to provide an aircraft.

Jacobsen was an experienced former DEA agent. He was the controlling agent for Barry Seal, who pled guilty to

132

federal drug smuggling charges and cooperation with DEA.

Under Jacobsen's direction, Seal piloted a C-123 military transport plane to a landing strip in Nicaragua. He and his crew secretly photographed Pablo Escobar, Jorge Ochoa, and Nicaraguan Sandinista officials loading cocaine onto the aircraft. Jacobsen was hoping to further the cocaine investigation and bring down the leadership of the Nicaraguan Government. Oliver North, a former USMC Lt. Colonel and national security advisor under President Reagan, allegedly leaked the photograph to the media. North wanted to boost support for the U.S. Government's effort to fund the Nicaraguan Contra Rebels in their plan to take control of the country.

After the photographs' leak, it forced DEA to arrest or indict the suspects in the investigation, compromising Barry Seal's role as a confidential informant.

Seal entered a guilty plea in federal court in Louisiana as part of his arrangement with the Government. Declining to enter the federal witness protection program against the federal prosecutor's recommendations, Seal signed his own death warrant. The court ordered Seal to serve his time in a halfway house in Louisiana.

Soon after he settled into the halfway house, Sicarios (Colombian drug cartel hitmen) ambushed Seal, killing him in a hail of gunfire. These guys played hardball, and I had no intention of losing my informants to them.

Jacobsen left DEA after being recruited by U.S. Customs Service Investigations in Mobile, Alabama. He developed one of the most successful undercover operations in the agency's history. In 1988, Congress subpoenaed Jacobsen to testify before the House Judiciary subcommittee on crime about the details of his investigation in Nicaragua.

Jacobsen said his partner, Ernie Winberg, would coordinate Operation Skymaster activities with our investigation in New York.

Winberg gave Dennis details on airplanes available for him to use for his flight to Colombia. Winberg said they had pilots and a navigator, also a mechanic who had worked with Barry Seal on many of Seal's trips for the government should we need them.

I later took him up on his offer, putting Jimmy Flack, the navigator, and Dale Edwards, the pilot, to work in New York. But that was all in the future.

All we had to do now is find Dennis an aircraft.

Dennis said Novak was expecting him to return to his apartment. He wrote down the telephone number of a public telephone near Novak's apartment and asked me to call the number in 45 minutes.

Over the next few hours, Dennis and I spoke several times to determine if the proper aircraft had been located. I contacted Customs Agent Nick Jacobellis, who operated Operation Blade Runner in Miami during the "Miami Vice Era." Jacobellis managed a fleet of undercover aircraft targeting drug smugglers. Planes they would use to fly drugs into Florida, where they would be arrested.

Jacobellis said his aircraft were short-range and needed refueling to travel from Colombia to New York. I passed the information on to Dennis. He said he'd go back to Novak's apartment to fill them in and call me later in the evening.

Around 9:00 PM, my pager went off with a number to call Dennis.

"I gave him the ten-grand back," Dennis said. "Novak will try to locate the plane and let me know."

This put our air smuggling investigation in a holding pattern. Could we actually put this together? Over the next few days, we would find out. What we would learn is that drug smugglers had unlimited resources, and the federal government did not.

Another major obstacle stood in our path. John Novak, using the name John Joyce, was a fugitive from justice. In the early 1980's he was convicted, along with Dennis, for smuggling marijuana. After his release from federal prison,

135

he developed a cocaine, marijuana, and Thai sticks (cannabis wrapped in a leafy cigar) distribution network on the west coast of the U.S. Novak was now under federal indictment for his part in a Continuing Criminal Enterprise. He could be facing over 20 years in federal prison.

We hoped the U.S. Marshals or another federal agency didn't arrest him during the next few months. It would cut our investigation short before we ever got a plane in the air. We would record no meetings with Novak in case he mentioned his status as a fugitive. We also chose not to tell the RAIC, Mike Nestor, or Ann Kenner, the Assistant United States Attorney assigned to our case. As far as they knew, we were investigating John Joyce, with no criminal record, and a convicted felon named Robert Krevsky.

A few days later, Novak contacted Dennis and asked him to return to New York. Dennis asked Novak what was up.

"I got some friends with the right piece of equipment," Novak said. "They need you to take a look. We'll need a place to park it on the island." Code words for a Fixed Based of Operations on Long Island.

Dennis and I were off to New York again. Carbonari and I dropped Dennis off a few blocks from Novak's apartment. Once again, he disappeared for twenty-four hours.

Operation Tobago

I received a call from Tony, who was in New York City for a few days on business. Carbonari and I had Dennis call Novak and tell him Tony was in the city.

Novak asked to call Tony on a public telephone. Dennis gave him the number at a phone booth at JFK Airport. When the phone rang, Dennis answered and handed it to Tony.

"Can you travel south with our friend?" Novak asked.

"Sure, I'm around," Tony answered.

"It's good to hear your voice. I'll have things worked out in the next two months, and we'll be good to go. Dennis will let you know when we're ready. Take care, man."

Novak hung up.

The four of us returned to the Customs Office in Bohemia to document the call and discuss the case.

Dennis and Tony signed agreements they would not enter the country of Cuba's airspace while traveling to Colombia. After completing any necessary authorizations for the pilots to travel to Colombia, we all went to a nearby restaurant.

After dinner, we dropped them at Tony's hotel in Manhattan. Carbonari and I left and let Tony and Dennis catch up on old times. I would pick Dennis up in the morning.

The following morning I met Dennis, who said he had spoken with Novak.

"He wants me to check out a location for an FBO (fixed-base of operations) for storing the plane," Dennis said. "I told him I had a place on Long Island I thought would work and would get back to him. He wanted Tony to check it out. I told him I'd take care of it."

U.S. Customs had a fixed-base operation at Westhampton Airport on Long Island code-named Operation "Tobago." Carbonari said this site would be perfect.

Kenny 'the Jamaican' was an excellent reliable informant with a pilot's license and an airplane he kept hangered at the Customs fixed-base operation. He also had a small office.

We introduced Dennis to Kenny, and they seemed to hit it off. Kenny showed him his airplane, a Cessna 402 twin-engine aircraft. Once they'd talked, Dennis felt comfortable bringing Kenny into the operation. He'd tell Novak he met Kenny when he tried to find an airplane to fly charters from Long Island to Cape Cod.

Dennis paged Novak, and Novak called within five

minutes.

"We went to see the place in Westhampton," Dennis told him. "It looks good."

"Great," Novak said. "I'll pick up Bobbie and meet you there."

"Okay, call this number when you're close," Dennis said, giving him the number for Kenny's office.

We figured we had at least ninety minutes to prepare for the meeting since Novak was still in Manhattan and had to pick up Krevsky.

Carbonari called Dave McAndrew and asked for a few agents to help cover this crucial meeting. McAndrew arranged for three agents to meet Carbonari and me at a gas station near the airport. Carbonari and I would make a video recording of the meeting while other agents monitored the movements of Novak and Krevsky.

John Murray, the U.S. Customs Service technical support officer, installed a concealed video camera and recorder in Kenny's office. Carbonari and I brought Dennis and Kenny together, and we discussed our plan for the meeting.

As we were testing the video, the office phone rang. Kenny answered and handed the phone to Dennis. Dennis repeated the conversation out loud for all to hear.

"Oh, you are here already. I didn't expect you for an hour."

Carbonari and I raced out of the office and into a small, adjacent, soundproofed room. We waited to activate the recording until Dennis returned with Novak and Krevsky.

Our hearts were pounding so hard we thought Novak and Krevsky would hear.

A short time later, Dennis came in with the two others. Carbonari activated the recording equipment, and it was showtime!

Novak, who stood approximately 5'9" with brown hair and slightly overweight, seemed very anxious.

"I didn't think you'd be here for at least an hour," Dennis said.

"Bobby was on his way to my apartment, and we decided to surprise you," Novak said, turning to eye Kenney. "After all, we don't know this guy."

Krevsky, 5' 10" with black hair and also slightly overweight, looked for a reaction.

Dennis introduced Kenny, then chatted them up with small talk, trying to defuse the tension.

"So, how do you know, Kenny? Novak asked, still wary of the new guy.

"I met Dennis about five years ago," Kenney said,

following the script we'd discussed. "He wanted to set up a charter service from Long Island to Cape Cod, Martha's Vineyard, and Nantucket. He came to me looking for a plane."

The ease of Kenny's explanation did the trick. Novak calmed down,

Kenny was like a cool breeze, directing Novak and Krevsky to the window in the office where they could see his Cessna 402 aircraft tied down on the ramp.

"I've been running a charter service for six years; everybody knows me here, so I can run under the radar. My plane has plenty of range, and I could add an extra fuel tank if I needed it."

"Can you fly a thousand pounds of weed from Jamaica back here?" Novak asked.

"Of course, I know the perfect route. But I'd want Dennis as my co-pilot."

Novak laughed. "You guys are both gonna be rich. You'll get fifty thousand for helping Dennis with this deal."

Krevsky chimed in. "And I've got connections in New York that could move as much coke and weed as he could get his hands on. Let me ask you something. Would a Westwind jet tied down next to your Cessna attract attention?"

"Nope, I park other planes here all the time. Nobody will even give it a moment's thought."

"Okay, once the Westwind is here," Novak said, "we'd like to make five or six trips a month to Colombia. Can you handle that?"

"Of course," Kenney said. "You wanna take a walk around and check out the aircraft parking area?"

Novak looked at Krevsky, then said, "Nah, we're good. Don't want to let anyone see us around here."

The men shook hands, and Novak and Krevsky headed back to the city.

Carbonari shut down the recording equipment. Outside surveillance units followed Novak and Krevsky as they left the airport, making sure they didn't stick around and try to run their own surveillance.

Kenny had passed the test with Novak, proving he could handle his role in this investigation.

Dennis stayed with Kenny as they had planned to take a test flight together in Kenny's airplane. Carbonari and I left with the videotape of the meeting. When we arrived at the U.S. Customs Office in Bohemia, we were greeted by Carbonari's Group supervisor, Dave McAndrew, and the RAIC of the office, Mike Nestor.

Nestor had two questions. Was the case still moving

along, and did we have any more identifying data on John Joyce (Novak).

"Joyce and Krevsky arrived at the West Hampton airport in a car registered to Sky Corp. It is Krevsky's company," Carbonari said. "We got nothing else definite on Joyce, but I think he bought Kenney's act. No doubt he'll put something together."

Nestor seemed relatively pleased the case was still on track. He wasn't overly concerned about the lack of identifying data on Joyce. While what Carbonari said wasn't the entire story, it wasn't complete bullshit either. We didn't have absolute identification of 'Joyce,' giving us a weasel way out when his identity became known.

When I played the videotape of the meeting, an overjoyed Nestor congratulated us on the investigation. Krevsky's and Novak's overt efforts to facilitate the importation of drugs, and the incriminating statements they made on the recording, were all indictable offenses. Anything more was a bonus.

Nestor knew little or nothing about the flow of an investigation. He only asked questions because somebody above him in the Customs food chain wanted answers. Nestor told us we would have to brief DEA's local office on the progress of our case. Mike Yaniello would be our contact at DEA.

Per a Memorandum of Understanding (MOU) between the U.S. Customs Service and DEA, all narcotics investigations conducted by Customs were coordinated with DEA. Also, the MOU required any investigation involving travel to Colombia by an agent, informant, airplane, or boat, DEA would get country clearance. DEA managed all U.S. operatives traveling into Colombian territory to further an investigation.

Because of political corruption in Colombia and cartel bribery of government officials, DEA would notify the U.S. Ambassador by secure cable. The cable would then kept in an embassy vault. The cable would be removed from the vault only if an agent, informant, airplane, or boat were detained by Colombian authorities while operating on behalf of the U.S. Government.

In such an event, the Ambassador would show the cable to Colombian authorities to secure the release of the designated U.S. agents or equipment. It was the proverbial 'Get out of jail free card,' only to be utilized as a last resort.

Carbonari knew Yaniello and said he was a good agent. He wouldn't ask questions about Novak's true identity. Carbonari and I agreed to keep Dennis away from Yaniello to make sure he didn't unwittingly give up Novak's fugitive status.

Fly Me to the Moon

During the second week of April, Novak asked Dennis to travel to New York for a meeting. This investigation was now a major priority of the New York and Boston field offices.

I had the U.S. Customs Air Wing for support, which made moving between the locations more efficient. One pilot, Brad Atkinson, and I became close. Brad had given me valuable intelligence on suspect aircraft at municipal airports in southeastern Massachusetts.

I called Brad and asked him if he could pick me up at New Bedford Municipal Airport, eight miles from my home, and then fly me to Hyannis Airport on Cape Cod to meet with Dennis. The three of us would then fly to MacArthur Airport in Islip, New York, to meet Carbonari.

I drove to New Bedford Airport and waited for the Air Wing's Cessna 310 aircraft. Brad was a retired military pilot, knowledgeable in aviation. I flew with him on aerial surveillance activities of organized crime figure Anthony Rizzo and others in the past.

He was a superb pilot.

A short time later, the aircraft landed, taxied over, and

146

Brad shut down the engines. I climbed aboard, and Brad had me sit in the co-pilot's seat, asking me if I was ready for my first flight lesson.

"I'll give it a try," I said, trying to calm the knot in my stomach. Atkinson gave me a quick lesson in the flight controls. He showed me how to accelerate, steer, and maintain a level trajectory.

"Ready to go, Russ?" he said, as he started first the left, then the right engines.

And we were off, Atkinson helping me taxi the aircraft to the end of the runway.

"Nothing to worry about," Atkinson said. "I haven't lost a student pilot... yet." He smiled.

The control tower gave us our clearance, I throttled up, and we were off, racing toward the end of the runway. Brad told me to move the throttle forward gently, and we gained speed rapidly as he adjusted the flaps. The plane lifted off the ground.

Once we cleared the trees at the end of the runway, he told me to push slightly forward until we leveled off. However, I pushed the throttle full-forward, and we ascended into a rapid climb.

Brad took control of the aircraft so it wouldn't stall out. Thankfully, he leveled the aircraft and helped me avoid my

147

first plane crash.

I thought that was it with my flying lessons, but I was wrong. Brad is a patient guy. He requested permission from the tower to land and try again. His instructions were perfect; we made a textbook approach and a flawless landing.

After landing, Brad requested clearance for another takeoff. I taxied the airplane to the runway, and this time got us airborne with no hiccups. Brad set our course for Hyannis Airport on Cape Cod in Massachusetts.

In a short time, we were making our approach to the runway in Hyannis. Brad let me take the plane in for its landing. I nailed a perfect touchdown and taxi to the terminal area, where Dennis was outside awaiting our arrival.

After a brief introduction, we were off again to New York.

Due to the congestion at this location and the size of the commercial passenger jets in the approach pattern, I let Brad land the plane. I did not want to chance a head-on collision with a Boeing 737 commercial passenger jet.

After landing and a short taxi to the hangar where the U.S. Customs Air Wing was located, Atkinson shut down the aircraft while Dennis and I met with Carbonari.

Once the aircraft was secured, we dropped Dennis at the

Carlyle Hotel. He would walk to Novak's apartment. We met Dennis the following day to discuss the details of his meeting with Novak.

The following morning, Dennis filled us in on his meeting with Novak.

At the apartment, Novak introduced Dennis to someone named David. David gave Dennis a brochure about an Israeli manufactured Westwind Wind I Jet. Dennis described David as slightly built, shorter than Novak, and soft-spoken. Novak told him David was a stockbroker and financial consultant. They had met Novak several years ago when they crossed paths in federal prison.

"Can you handle the Westwind?" Novak asked.

"Sure, no problem," Dennis replied.

"Okay, David's using a company owned by Krevsky's brother, Daniel. It's called Hercules Construction, and they'll lease the jet and provide a place to store it at Westhampton Airport."

Daniel Krevsky and Rapaport signed a monthly contract with an aircraft leasing company in Delaware for a Westwind 1 jet for $40,000 per month.

The sale of two kilos of coke a month would cover their cost to lease the aircraft. As soon as the jet was in their possession, the Colombians were ready to supply enough coke for at least six trips per month. Novak told Dennis they would pay him one million dollars per flight.

"I'll need a co-pilot," Dennis said.

"Is our friend from the college (FCI Danbury) Tony available? We can trust him."

"I'll try and talk him out of retirement. He was in the city a few days ago."

"Tell him you'll split the million for the first trip, but I'll kick in an extra 5ook for the second one."

"What about all these college grads being on the lease documents?" Dennis asked. "That might draw attention."

"No worries. Krevsky's brother, Dan, is clean, and it's his name on the lease. He also has a company called Sky Corp we can use.

"Once your Jamaican friend, Kenny, signs his part of the lease agreement, the aircraft will go to Westhampton Airport."

"Will Kenny pay for any of the monthly cost?"

"All the costs—insurance, maintenance, everything—are included in the lease price," David said. "It costs him nothing. Have him send me all his corporate documents, and I'll take care of the paperwork."

With the details worked out, Novak gave Dennis $2,000. He told him to give Kenny $1000 and keep the rest for his expenses. The following morning Dennis left Novak's apartment and called me from a public phone.

"Get a cab," I said. "We'll meet you at the New York Port Authority."

Carbonari and I headed over to the Port Authority. Dennis filled us in on the details of meeting with Novak as we drove to Kenny's fixed-base operation at West Hampton Airport.

Kenny faxed the paperwork required for the Westwind jet's lease to David, and he'd return the lease contract to Kenny for his approval. Dennis contacted David and informed him that Kenny was all set.

David said Westlease would deliver the aircraft the following week. Dave McAndrew joined us at Kenny's office. He asked to speak with us outside.

"The SAC of the U.S. Customs New York Field Office was willing to support this investigation with all of the resources available," McAndrew said. "The Commissioner of the U.S. Customs Service was receiving daily updates on this investigation and forwarding to the U.S. Secretary of the Treasury along with Vice President George H. Bush. This case is drawing major interest."

"Dave," I said, "if this case would have been closed already if the management in the Boston office had handled it. They are nowhere near as aggressive as you guys."

McAndrew chuckled. "Mike Nestor, the RAC (RAIC,) will oversee the case. But keep in mind he always worries about his own ass. Keep the details between us, or he'll shut it down before we ever get off the ground.

"I'll have Kenny bring Dennis to a local hotel for the evening and check you into a nearby hotel for the evening."

Carbonari said he would meet us later.

Mc Andrew brought me to the Islander Hotel. After I checked in, he invited me for a few drinks with Carbonari and some guys from their office. Once the war stories were over, it was time to head back to the hotel.

With the lease arrangement all set, McAndrew said I should head back to Boston, and he'd arrange for Dennis to fly home on a commercial flight. I called my favorite pilot, Brad Atkinson. The following day, he flew me back to New Bedford on a U.S. Customs helicopter.

I was getting my fill of flight time, hoping to keep this case alive and not getting derailed by the resistance to proactive investigations. Dealing with the bad guys was hard enough; fighting internal agency inertia was downright exasperating.

Play Ball, Mr. Vice President

On Monday, I returned to my office in Boston to complete some paperwork for my travel and a detailed Investigative Report for my Group Supervisor, Jim Burke.

The only comment I got from him was, "Is this case ever going to happen"?

I shook my head. "Why don't you just get updates from New York?"

"You know," he said, "if the case was being run out of Boston, you'd probably get a promotion to a GS-13."

I was a GS-12 (government pay grades are designated by GS-); getting a promotion to a GS 13 in Boston was difficult for an outsider who had come to the office from another agency.

"Well, we are a federal agency, and Boston didn't want any part of running this case. It shouldn't matter if the case is run out of another office. The case is complex, whether it's run from here Boston or New York."

He shrugged his shoulders. "You know how things are run here. They have their favorites. If this case doesn't materialize, they will never let you work on something like this again."

"No shit. I'm leaving for New York tomorrow. I'll keep you in the loop as the case develops."

Come Tuesday, I was off to New York again. I arranged for Brad Atkinson to pick Dennis up in Hyannis and bring him to MacArthur Airport. I would meet them there.

On my drive to New York, I often listened to Sports talk radio, and New York had the best show on the air, WFAN. I was a big baseball fan, and the Boston Red Sox were my favorite team.

It was opening day for the New York Mets. The team and the fans were still reveling in their 1986 World Series Championship victory over the Red Sox made possible by the ball that rolled through Bill Buckner's legs in game 6.

The Mets were down to their last strike, nobody on base, and losing by two runs in the bottom of the 10th inning.

After staging a comeback for the ages and tying the game at 5, a slow-rolling ground ball caromed between Buckner's legs, allowing the winning run to score, and the Mets took game six. The stunning comeback propelled them to a blowout win in game 7, denying the Red Sox a chance to win their first World Series Championship since 1918.

I still vividly recall all the details of the game to this very day. I had been to game five of that series and watch the Red Sox take a 3-2 game advantage needing only one more to win the series. Tickets were being sold for $1000 a piece, so a friend and I used our Master Tins (ID Badge) at the gate and found great seats.

We often referred to our badge and credentials as Master Tin, because like Mastercard, it was accepted everywhere. Not strictly kosher, but one of the few perks of the job.

I still vividly recall all the details of the game.

I had just crossed the New York state border on Interstate 95 heading south. I tuned in to WFAN, the home of the New Mets radio broadcast of their games, and, much to my surprise, there was a pregame special being carried for the home opener of the New York Mets.

The Vice President of the United States, George H. W. Bush, would be in attendance and throw out the first pitch. My mind churned with a plan to attend the ballgame.

I had become acquainted with several of the Special Agents from the U.S. Secret Service during the 1980 Presidential Campaign. On one assignment with the Secret Service, I was part of the security detail for former CIA Director and then-Republican Presidential Candidate, George H. W. Bush.

My assignment that day was the holding room. This area is designated as a secure location; the candidate would be escorted from his motorcade and prepare for his speech at the hotel convention room.

After the speech and media questions and answer period, the candidate would return to the room. I would oversee the U.S. Army Explosives Ordinance Detail (EOD) team conducting a sweep of the hotel room for explosives. Once they completed the sweep, I secured the room.

The radio chirped; Bush was on his way.

I unlocked the door to the room and placed the key above the doorframe as instructed. As Mr. Bush arrived, I opened the door and stepped back. He stopped to greet me; my heart was pounding in my chest.

He asked if the men on the detail were hungry.

"Yes, sir. We are," was all I could say.

His reaction astounded me.

Turning to the head of his campaign staff, he told him to order some cheese, crackers, fruit, and some soft drinks for the guys that "keep me safe."

The staffer ordered the food as Mr. Bush went inside the holding room.

Mr. Bush came out of the doorway preceded by his staff, then stopped to tell me he ordered the food, and he would return with a surprise. The staff and future Vice President departed, surrounded by agents from the protection detail.

The food arrived on cue, and the Secret Service Agent

who had joined me earlier said agents from the motorcade would join us to chow down. About an hour had passed, we received an alert Mr. Bush was finishing with media questions and would return to the room in a few minutes.

We cleaned up the room, and then I waited outside the door; Mr. Bush once again stopped in the doorway, reached in his jacket pocket, and out came jellybean mints. He said they were one of his favorites and handed some to the agents.

The future President asked if I was a Red Sox fan, then told me he had become an avid Texas Rangers fan and was hopeful they would compete with the Red Sox soon. I agreed and told the former Director of the CIA I would look forward to it.

Mr. Bush was one of the kindest and most cordial politicians I ever met while protecting Presidential candidates. I would never forget my first encounter with the United States' future President and hoped it would not be my last.

Taking my chances by using my "tin" to get into the opening day game, it was my good fortune to sit behind the Vice President. We were in a place we both had a common passion, a Major League baseball game. Who knew we would meet again at a baseball game of all places?

One agent I knew from the campaign detail took good

care of me. I took my seat as the Vice President passed by and watched him throw the ceremonial first pitch to the New York Mets All-Star catcher Gary Carter. The Vice President had been a standout first baseman during his collegiate career at Yale University and still had quite an arm.

After throwing the opening day pitch, the Vice President walked back to his box seat located right in front of mine. As he passed, the agent I knew told him I was the Customs agent assigned to the holding room at his campaign stop in Portsmouth, New Hampshire.

"Nice to see you again," he said.

"It is my honor, Mr. Vice President."

He took his seat, leaned back, and said. "No place I'd rather be."

"Me as well, sir."

The agents assigned to the detail raved about the treatment they received from the Vice President and his wife Barbara, and their family.

After a few innings, I left the ballpark and headed to the U.S. Customs Airwing in McArthur Airport. I met Dennis, Carbonari, and McAndrew. I told Dennis to call Rapaport from a public telephone and check on the aircraft's delivery status.

Rapaport told Dennis everything was on schedule, and

delivery was on for the following afternoon. The pilots transporting the aircraft would give him some brief instruction, then depart by helicopter back to their home base. Rapaport said he had completed a lease for the plane for $40,000 per month. Dennis told him he would confirm the delivery and fax any required paperwork to his office.

Finally, the big day had come.

It was a beautiful April day as the sun shone brightly through scattered clouds on deep blue early spring sky. Small groups of seagulls scattered above as they circled from the Hampton Beach shoreline.

I sat in my car on a side road facing the Westhampton Airport with binoculars in hand as the thunderous sound of jet engines roared above. A beautiful white jet broke through the clouds on its descent to the runway.

Chills sent shivers down my arms as my heart pounded. I broke into a sweat. I could just barely make out the aircraft tail number, N68WW, as its wheels touched down. The engines' sound changed as the reverse engine thrust brought the aircraft to a stop at the far end of the runway. Making a sharp turn onto the taxiway, the plane made its way toward the terminal.

I radioed the other surveillance units, "The Eagle has landed." Not the most original line, but the adrenaline was intense. I was one giant step closer to making a drug bust of historic proportions.

From my vantage point, I watched Dennis greet the pilots. They gave Dennis a quick run-through on the aircraft, then got into a vehicle parked on the ramp and left.

It was now Dennis's baby to fly.

Carbonari, McAndrew, and I went to Kenny's office to meet our undercover pilot. Dennis said that the aircraft was in pristine condition. The delivery pilots said the contract required certified type-rated pilots to operate the aircraft. Daniel Krevsky had signed as the responsible party; however, neither Dennis nor Tony Nargi had an active FAA Airmen's Certification. Both were suspended on their convictions for a federal offense. Even if they were active, neither had a current type rating to operate the aircraft.

Krevsky was responsible for pilot certifications, but the government ultimately shared some liability should the aircraft have an accident while under the U.S. Customs Service's control.

Carbonari shook his head in disbelief. "Now what?" he said.

Never one to get sidelined by an insurmountable obstacle, I contacted Jake Jacobsen, the agent running the other UC operation.

"Jake, Russ Protentis, I need a pilot rated to fly a Westwind jet for a case." I put the phone on speaker so everyone could hear.

"Hmm, I got just the guy," Jake said. "Guy's name is Dale. He's a good ole' boy, probably never been to New York. If you can keep him away from the hookers in Times' Square, he's your man."

The hooker line got a laugh out of everyone.

"One problem, though," Jake said.

"What's that?" I asked.

"You'll have to cover his travel expenses. Do that, and I'll have him on the next plane up there."

McAndrew gave me the thumbs up.

"I'll send you the travel authorizations tomorrow," I said and hung up.

Problem solved; we had our pilot.

Pablo Escobar and the Super Model

That evening, Novak summoned Dennis to his apartment to discuss his upcoming journey to Colombia. Novak said Pablo Escobar's Medellin Cartel would monitor the trip. They would divide the coke evenly between the New York people from Escobar's group and Jorge Ochoa.

Escobar and Ochoa were the founders of the Medellin Cocaine Cartel centered in Medellin, Colombia. Coincidently Escobar, the cartel leader, started his criminal career stealing cars and smuggling contraband in the U.S.

Escobar adapted his methods for smuggling contraband cigarettes to transport marijuana and cocaine out of Colombia into neighboring countries and eventually to his biggest customer, the United States.

During the 1980s, the cartel made an estimated $420,000,000 every week. This cartel distributed 80% of the world's cocaine—exporting fifteen tons daily—landing Escobar on the Forbes list of billionaires from 1987 to 1993, with an estimated net worth of twenty-five billion dollars.

162

Novak said the Medellin Cartel wanted to open a route by air from Colombia directly to New York to avoid law enforcement in the southern United States. Ochoa would handle the distribution of cocaine transported into New York.

Dennis would recruit a crew of pilots to operate additional planes for this operation. After each jet made three successful trips, they would exchange it for another plane to avoid the Feds' attention. Novak said they would secure a suitable runway in Colombia within the next two weeks and make at least two trips a week.

Spreading an aviator's map on the apartment floor, Novak pointed to Santa Marta, Colombia, for the potential landing point. Gus said he needed assurances from Dennis that the plane could make the journey from Santa Marta to Long Island, NY, without refueling.

"It's possible," Dennis said, "but unlikely with 1000 kilos of cargo onboard. But I have a solution. We can install a small reserve tank and transfer the fuel to the main tank inflight.

"Can you take care of getting the tank?" Novak asked.

"No problem, I got a friend who can install it for me. But there's another issue. I definitely need a co-pilot to assist in the trip.

"Can you get Tony?"

"I can try. But in the interim, I got somebody with experience on this plane. He'll help familiarize me with the aircraft."

Dennis left the meeting and filled in Carbonari and me on the details. We knew we had some extraordinary work to do to complete this operation. The following day, I contacted Jake Jacobsen at his office and asked if he could assist in this crazy situation.

Jacobsen said he would send Dale on the next plane to work with us.

Jacobsen also said he had an airplane mechanic, Jimmy Flack, skilled in these operations. Jimmy—who'd done repairs for and flown with Barry Seal—was available, but not for at least 10 days. I decided it would work to our advantage; we didn't want to jump at every request made by Novak and his crew. It might cause them to think Dennis was a government agent. Who else could meet every demand immediately?

Patience and caution—pushing back on rushing headlong in these things—would play more effectively in establishing our credibility.

First things first, I received authorization to bring Dale Edwards to New York. When he arrived at La Guardia, my first impression was a pleasant Georgia boy who boasted of a half dozen journeys into the jungles of Colombia in a variety of airplanes.

True to form, the first thing he wanted to know was how to get to Times Square. I changed the subject and asked about his experiences flying to Colombia.

Dale said he took two flights there for dopers before cooperating with U.S. Customs; the last four were for Operation Skymaster. Dale said he had survived hair-raising journeys in and out of some of the most remote runways in Colombia. He would shave his head or grow a beard to change his appearance for each flight in the event he encountered the same loading crews in the jungle.

He said he never drew suspicion from the folks on the ground, unlike some of his co-pilots. On his last journey for the dopers, a loading crew leader recognized the pilot seated next to him, and the crew grabbed him from the plane while others held Dale. What followed nearly gave him heart failure. The crew tied the co-pilot face down to a fallen tree trunk as he begged for mercy. After several minutes of gruesome torture, the screams fell silent.

They interrogated Dale about his association with the other pilot. He told them the guy hired him the day before by phone. That's all he knew.

The leader looked at Dale, uncertain if he could trust him yet unwilling to cancel the flight.

"You're flying home alone. Finish loading the plane and get out of here."

Dale begged for his co-pilot's release to no avail. The leader, covered with blood, gave Dale one of the co-pilot's fingers with a ring attached. He said the guy flew a plane carrying 250 kilos of cocaine to Miami that turned out to be part of a government sting operation. He said his cousin was arrested and was now in federal prison in the U.S. The guy had to pay.

They gave Dale a piece of paper with a telephone number written on it and told him to contact the number when he landed. The flight arrangements were changed, and he was told to fly the aircraft to a different airport than planned.

Overwhelmed and shaking during the entire flight, he decided it was time to turn his life around before it was too late. Upon landing in southern Florida, he contacted the U.S. Customs Service. They turned Dale's harrowing trip into a successful sting operation of a known narcotics trafficker. Unfortunately, it was too late for his co-pilot to change his lifestyle, and Dale never saw him again. I asked Dale to keep that story between us and not tell Dennis.

He agreed.

Over the next week, Dale and Dennis took several test flights, and Dale raved about Dennis's ability to handle aircraft. Meanwhile, I contacted Tony, who would be visiting the U.S. for the next three weeks, arriving at JFK Airport from Switzerland in the next few days.

Tony asked if I had any contact with an FAA-certified flight instructor as he needed to reactivate his pilot's license. He wanted to start soon as his employer would give him the time because they wanted him to fly training aircraft. I told him we might have a side trip to Colombia for some extra money. He said he was interested and would love to fly for the U.S. government again.

As Dennis and Dale continued to familiarize themselves with the Westwind jet, I headed for JFK Airport to meet Tony. As a Customs agent, I had the clearance to enter the passenger arrival gate and baggage area for investigative purposes and greet cooperating witnesses.

I entered the gate area for Swiss Air with a veteran Customs Inspector and waited for Tony to come down the ramp. I noticed several other people waiting for a dignitary. There was also a large gathering of media outside the exit of the U.S. Customs examination area.

I knew the gathering was not for Tony.

Stepping out from the throng passengers entering the area to be processed for entry to the U.S. was one of the most beautiful women in the world. I heard one of the adoring Customs Inspectors say that's Elle Macpherson. McPherson, the reigning cover girl for Sports Illustrated, was escorted by her agent and the airline crew to a segregated inspection area.

As I gazed at the world-famous Australian beauty, Tony tapped me on the shoulder, chuckled, and said, "I thought you were here for me."

Tony said the whole plane was buzzing about the beautiful woman seated in first class. Seeing her walk by me, I could understand the buzz. She is a striking woman.

After a moment, I came to my senses. The Customs Inspector escorted Tony and me to the Supervisors area. He asked if Tony had anything to declare, had him sign the Customs Declaration Form, and told us to have a nice day.

I brought Tony up to date on the plane leased by Novak and his associates and asked if he could handle the journey from Colombia to New York.

Tony said to count him as a ready and willing volunteer. He asked when we would be needed for this flight, and I told him most likely not for a few weeks. He asked about the FAA flight instructor, and I told him I had started the process.

It just so happened I worked out with an FAA instructor

named Lou Higgins. I gave Higgins a full explanation of Tony's background and the need for confidentiality. With a letter from the SAC of U.S. Customs in Boston, I got a waiver for Tony's federal conviction so he could begin his recertification immediately.

Higgins said he read Nargi's war record in the archives of the U.S. Navy and would do everything he could to help the decorated Vietnam War Veteran. He agreed to work around Tony's schedule and, if he passed the course, would renew his airmen's certificate as a priority.

Tony was elated. He said he would make the flight to Colombia for free. As in many other instances in my career, I often saw God's hand in helping me overcome insurmountable obstacles in my path. This was another one of those instances.

Tony stayed overnight in New York and met with Dennis and me over dinner to discuss our plans. Tony said he had an important meeting to attend in Switzerland for his employer during the second week of May. Still, he would be available any other time to make the flight to Colombia.

The following morning Tony was off to Massachusetts, where he would meet with Lou Higgins and regain his airmen's certificate. It didn't take long for Higgins to judge Tony more than qualified. He passed all the tests and his

169

inflight examination with flying colors. I thanked Higgins for his time and effort and promised him dinner at a restaurant of his choice soon. Higgins said he was proud to be of service in the war on drugs and would follow our investigation's progress.

As the days passed, Novak updated Dennis on their flight's anticipated date and possible landing location in Colombia. Dale returned to Alabama and said he would return when required.

Dennis met with Novak, who insisted on avoiding refueling and making the journey without an interim stop. Novak asked Dennis to install an extra tank in the aircraft to fly non-stop from Colombia to New York.

"I'll need to make some calls," Dennis said, heading outside to a public telephone to fill me in about Novak's insistence for an additional fuel tank. Novak's paranoia about cops discovering him worked to our advantage, giving Dennis the perfect excuse to keep us informed.

I contacted Jake and asked if he could send his mechanic to New York. He agreed to send Jimmy. Dennis returned to Novak's apartment and told him the mechanic would arrive the following day.

"Money is no problem," Novak said, handing Dennis $3700 to cover the cost of the extra fuel tank. "As long as the plane can fly non-stop, that's all that matters."

*****

It was another beautiful spring day at LaGuardia Airport. Jimmy came out of the domestic terminal and met Carbonari and me curbside. A slender man with a brown beard and heavy British accent, Jimmy was a likable chap. He said he was licking his chops for a hot dog with sauerkraut, a New York City street vendor specialty. Carrying a bag of tools—something he brought wherever he traveled—he jumped in the car, and we headed off.

I treated Jimmy to some Nathan's Hotdogs with the works—generous piles of mustard and sauerkraut slathered on—which he said was everything he imagined. Carbonari and I brought Jimmy to his hotel, where we introduced him to Dennis. Dennis then invited us to join him at the restaurant next to the hotel for roast duck and champagne compliments of John Novak.

"I'll drink to that," Jimmy said, and off we went.

After a few drinks, Jimmy rattled on about his friendship with Barry Seal. He regaled us with the story of how he installed and operated a hidden camera in a C-123 military transport. They used the camera to take photographs of the Nicaraguan Minister of the Interior standing alongside Pablo

Escobar and Jorge Ochoa overseeing the loading of kilo bricks of cocaine into the aircraft. These photographs revealed a direct link between the Nicaraguan government and the Medellin Cartel.

In our case, Jimmy would just install an auxiliary reserve tank—known by smugglers as a bladder—to ensure the aircraft's direct return to Long Island from Colombia. He would begin his bladder tank install in the morning.

In the way these cases go, chance intervened and almost derailed the case before we got off the ground. Several airport employees called local and state police and the FBI to report suspicious activity—flashlights and the buzzing sound of a Sawzall—inside a multi-million-dollar jet. We intervened with the law enforcement agencies after some quick explanations and averted disaster.

Three days later, mission accomplished, Jimmy was on his way back to Alabama. Days dragged into weeks, but we were ever so close to takeoff. In these cases, things outside our control can shut them down without warning.

Interagency conflicts, instability near the landing strip in Colombia, investigative targets arrested by another agency, information leaks or unreliable informants, and the number one obstacle, loss of confidence by the U.S. Customs Service, often compromise cases.

A common theme by the hierarchy in U.S. Customs in Boston was "Big cases, big problems. Little cases, little problems. No cases, no problems." But I had growing confidence the U.S. Customs Service offices on Long Island and New York City had the hutzpah to make this happen. I became a believer in my father's favorite Sinatra tune. "If I can make it there, I'll make it anywhere. It's up to you New York, New York."

Because of the attention caused by the bladder installation, Novak suggested Dennis take the jet for a ride to another state and keep it there for a few days. Keeping me in mind, he suggested the municipal airport in New Bedford, MA.

Novak agreed.

I had not been home for several weeks and missed my wife and children, so I took a ride. The ride was amazing. Dennis had mastered the operation of this multi-million-dollar aircraft. Twenty-two minutes after wheels went up on the plane in Westhampton, we touched down in New Bedford, MA.

After a perfect three-point landing, the plane taxied gently to the hangar. Dennis shut down the aircraft, and we went out of the gate where my wife and children were waiting with open arms. Dennis's girlfriend waited in his

Jaguar to bring him home.

Two days later, we were off again to Westhampton for the monthly maintenance check we had arranged at McArthur Islip Airport on Long Island. We took twenty-four minutes on the return because of a strong headwind. Dennis introduced me as his friend. I would do my best to distract the maintenance contractor from the area below the rear seat where the bladder tank had been installed. The inspection was completed without flaw, and Dennis piloted the aircraft back to West Hampton. Brad Atkinson drove me to my government car in Bohemia.

Things were looking promising.

From Cape Cod to Colombia

Things were quiet on Friday, so I had Dennis tell Novak he was returning to Massachusetts for the weekend to see his girlfriend. As a cover, Dennis said he would use the trip to make sure the plane was not under government surveillance.

Novak thought it was a brilliant idea. I also saw an opportunity to fly up front once again.

I asked Dennis to plot a course near New York City so I could see the city skyline. He notified the FAA of our trip to New Bedford and filed a plan to take us past Manhattan. Seated in the co-pilot seat with a front-row view was breathtaking. I decided, as soon as I had time, I would get my airmen's certificate.

We touched down in New Bedford in a flash. Dennis said he thought Novak would send the plane to Colombia soon, and he wanted me to contact Tony. I called Tony, who was back in Switzerland and stuck there until Saturday.

Fate intervened once again.

Just as we landed, Dennis got a pager alert to call Novak at his favorite public telephone. Novak, speaking in code, said he had the address (coordinates) for the parking garage down south (Colombia), and the sneakers (cocaine) were waiting.

Tony was unavailable for at least two days, so I called Jake Jacobsen to ask for Dale to fly with Dennis. Unfortunately, Dale was on a trip to Jamaica to pick up cocaine for Operation Skymaster; he was unavailable for three days.

When I told Dennis, he said he didn't know how to break it to Novak. I told him to keep it simple, tell the truth. I stood beside Dennis while he called Novak at the phone booth, which had become the main line of his de facto mobile office.

The sound of the operator-assisted call and quarters dropping into the phone added to the stress of the call. Something unfamiliar in today's cellular-infested world. But then it was the nature of the smuggling business.

Dennis first told him "Alabama" (Dale) was unavailable for three days, and Tony was in Europe for the next few days.

Novak initially sounded upset but then said he didn't trust Alabama. He knew Tony personally; knew he was a standup guy and would tell Gus he wanted to wait for Tony. Dennis told him Tony would arrive in Boston on Sunday evening, and they would leave for Colombia from New Bedford. The flight to New Bedford made Novak confident no law enforcement agency was watching them.

Dennis laid out the logistics for the flight.

"We'll fly to the Caribbean and refuel there, arriving down south on Tuesday."

"Great," Novak said. "Call me once you get back to Long Island unless something happens."

"Okay, we will."

"Got a pen?"

"Yup, shoot."

"11°07'10"N 74°13'50"W / 11.11944°N 74.23056°W. Use the call sign El Tigre, the ground crew will respond 'Westwind.'"

The coordinates identified their destination. Novak said the ground crew would direct them from Santa Marta International Airport to a remote landing strip less than two nautical miles from the airport.

The trip was on.

Dennis hung up the phone, and we both breathed a sigh of relief. I called Brad Atkinson and gave him the coordinates, which he said were in the coastal area of Santa Marta, Colombia.

I contacted Carbonari, who said DEA had granted country clearance for the trip. The pilots needed to depart for Colombia the following Monday, May 16th, and arrive in Santa Marta on May 17th. I told Carbonari that Tony was coming into Boston on Sunday, May 15th. I would get him a hotel room, and he would be rested for takeoff the following day.

It would turn out, as the trip unfolded with unexpected twists and turns, he would need it.

I notified a friend in the U.S. Customs Office in San Juan, Puerto Rico. Benjamin Garcia, I would be sending a plane and two pilots to San Juan on Monday evening. They would refuel and then fly to Colombia to pick up a "load." Garcia said he would be on vacation but would arrange for an agent from his office to meet the pilots in San Juan and ensure everything went off with no problems.

Garcia and I became close when I helped him relocate a witness from a significant heroin smuggling investigation to Boston. We met in December 1985 at an Intelligence school at the Federal Law Enforcement Training Center in Glynco, Georgia.

In October 1986, Garcia asked if I could babysit a witness and his family relocated temporarily north of Boston until his office brought a heroin smuggling investigation to trial. I agreed, and he handed the witness off to me in Boston.

I spent a week in December 1986 on the beaches of Old San Juan riding the waves while the witness testified in federal court. I returned the witness to Boston and moved him and his family to the north shore of Massachusetts. Garcia said he was indebted for bailing him out. The time had arrived for him to return the favor.

It seemed like all systems were leading us to a perfect trip to Colombia.

My family and I spent a quiet Sunday morning at Worship Service at Mullein Hill Baptist Church in Lakeville, Massachusetts, where I was a Deacon. During prayer requests, I asked the church body to pray for safe passage and a successful journey for all those involved in an investigation conducted by my agency.

After the service, I had lunch with my family, dropped them off at home, then headed to Logan Airport to meet Tony, who was arriving on Swissair from Zurich. Tony was going out of his way to help us complete this mission. Gainfully employed with a reputable international defense contractor, he used his own time to work with us, taking a week's vacation to fly this mission.

I met him at the gate and escorted him through the Customs area. We drove to the hotel I had reserved in Middleboro, Massachusetts. I briefed Tony on the details of the trip. He said he was ready for his 153rd combat mission.

We had a quick dinner, and I told him I would send a cab for him in the morning. I arranged for John Donnelly, an agent in the Customs Office in Boston, to drive Dennis from Hyannis to New Bedford.

It was May 16th, 1988, a beautiful mid-spring day as the sun shone brightly through the broken clouds on the nose of the sparkling Westwind 1 jet. My wife Lynda drove me to the New Bedford Airport with our son Nicholas, age five, and Lauren, age three, in the back seat.

Lynda was a real trooper. Six months pregnant with our daughter Alecia, suffering from a hernia and a torn rib cartilage throughout the pregnancy, she wanted to see me off on my flight to New York.

Tony arrived in a taxi as I was unbuckling Nicholas and Lauren from their car seats. Agent Donnelly pulled into the airport parking lot with Dennis moments later. I introduced my family to Tony and Dennis. They led my son Nicholas and daughter Lauren to the jet and asked if they wanted to take a seat in the cockpit.

They were overjoyed.

This aircraft was much larger than Nicholas's model airplanes, and my children received a quick course in jet aviation. Nicholas and Lauren wanted to strap themselves in the pilot's seats and practice a takeoff. As my children reached for the instrument panel, we decided the class was over, and it was time to say goodbye. After I embraced my family and said our goodbyes, Nicholas and Lauren told Dennis and Tony they would pray for them to have a safe trip to Colombia.

As my family headed back to the parking lot, Dennis, Tony, and I strapped into the upholstered leather seats onboard the aircraft. Dennis and Tony ran their checklists, touched a few buttons, flipped some switches, and then I noticed a look of deep concern on both their faces. The bewildered pilots took off their headsets and fumbled around with the instrument panel while reading the aircraft's operating manual.

The instrument panel had gone dark, and even I knew we had a problem. Dennis told Tony he had flown the aircraft several times without a hitch, including a recent flight where he gave me a skyline sunset view of Manhattan.

There was nothing I could do but pray.

Tony said he might have an answer. He clenched his fist and struck the top of the instrument panel, which lit up like a Christmas tree. There is nothing like a little old-fashioned nudge to revive an uncooperative aircraft.

The three of us could breathe again as the engines revved as if celebrating with us. Dennis contacted the control tower and informed them of our destination, Long Island MacArthur Airport. Taxiing to the far end of the runway, we prepared for takeoff. The control tower gave us a go—the sound of the jet engines revving up music to my ears—and we lifted off as an eagle in flight.

After landing at McArthur Airport, we met Carbonari and Atkinson. They would coordinate with the U.S. Customs Airwing in Florida to track the flight to Colombia and back to Long Island. Atkinson worked with Dennis and Tony to chart their flight path to Puerto Rico. He then faxed a copy to the U.S. Customs Service southeastern U.S. Airwing based in Jacksonville, Florida.

After several hours of planning, I called the San Juan Puerto Rico office and gave them the Westwind tail number, N68WW. I told them the plane would arrive at their location for refueling at around midnight. The agent assured me everything was all set.

Famous last words.

I watched the aircraft climb out, heading toward the New York skyline, then went to my hotel. I would wait there for the call from the pilots telling me they were leaving San Juan for Santa Marta, Colombia. Time ticked by, crawling along as I imagined all sorts of disastrous events.

Eventually, I fell asleep.

The pulsating sound of the room telephone interrupted my deep sleep. It was after midnight. Fumbling for the receiver, I heard Tony's voice with Dennis in the background. I was expecting Tony to tell me the plane was ready to take off for Colombia. Instead, Tony told me they had landed in San Juan. There was nobody in sight at the airport and no U.S. Customs agents around to meet them.

Tony told me he contacted the Southeastern Customs Communications Center to reach the Customs agent assigned to meet them. They told Tony the agent was off duty and on military leave. I tried frantically to contact any agent in the office who would be awake at that hour but to no avail. Planning to stay Monday night in San Juan and depart for Colombia on Tuesday morning, Tony and Dennis found a hotel room nearby.

But everything worked out fine. An agent from the San Juan office met Dennis and Tony in the morning and refueled the plane. The pilots, ready for takeoff, notified the tower they would be on a sightseeing flight, then left U.S. airspace for Santa Marta.

Everything that could go wrong did go wrong up to this point. We were hopeful the rest of the journey would be much smoother. Yet we faced more hopes dashed.

Once in Colombian airspace, if they failed to make radio contact or find the clandestine landing strip, they had enough fuel—thanks to the bladder tank—to land at several major airfields in Colombia.

On the way to the other field, they would devise a story that would keep them out of jail and allow us to contact the U.S. Embassy. Through my contacts there, they had a get-out-of-jail-free card.

Tony Nargi

After several hours of flying toward South America, we were about to approach Colombian air space. Dennis had flown a plane to Colombia to pick up marijuana and could speak a little Spanish. I was sure we would have our plane stolen because of supply and demand.

Colombia had an overwhelming supply of cocaine, and the U.S. had insatiable demand. Getting one to the other was a logistics nightmare. Pablo Escobar and the Medellin Cartel had a significant need for reliable transportation to deliver their product to the U.S. Our plane was something they both wanted and needed. Taking it from us at the cost of a couple of American pilots was hardly an obstacle.

As we passed from the Pacific Coast to inland Colombia, dense and patchy late morning fog limited visibility on the Santa Marta Airport approach. I tried to contact the ground, calling out "El Tigre" to "Westwind."

The response was immediate. Relieved we'd made contact, I still worried about what might happen on the ground.

They directed us due east of the main airport. We spotted the clandestine runway in a large open area, but fog covered the approach from the south. The pilots also saw a truck and small shack on the north end of the strip.

Because of the minimum approach speed of the aircraft and poor visibility, we made the final approach from the north, where there was a large opening in the layer of fog.

After a deep breath, Dennis took the plane in, landed, and came to a complete stop just short of the tree line at the end.

There was no room to turn the aircraft around under power. Dennis disengaged the nose wheel, shut down the engine, had the ground crew lift the nose end, and rotate the plane into position for takeoff. The supplier's crew had done this before, judging by their efficiency.

Ten men on the ground crew swarmed the plane. Dennis and I left the cockpit and were greeted by a man who identified himself as Angel. A pickup truck loaded with fifty-five gallon fuel drums approached and began refueling the plane.

It was apparent this was not the first time.

From a shack near the tree line about thirty or forty feet off the runway, several more men formed a fire brigade line. They loaded large canvas bags containing individual plastic-wrapped kilo bricks of cocaine into the passenger area. After the duffel bags were onboard, loose kilo bricks of cocaine wrapped in yellow rubber sleeves and clear plastic wrap followed.

Several names were written in black marker or marked by multicolored stickers on each brick, the most popular name being 'Gordos.'

Dennis halted the refueling at a little more than half, knowing the jet would refuel in the Grand Cayman Islands. Angel, who spoke broken English, said they had more than one ton to load. I told Angel we'd have to leave some behind due to the runway's length; too much weight would restrict our ability to clear the tree line at the opposite end.

"When you come back for more?" Angel asked.

"Three days," I said.

"We got this strip for this trip because we didn't know if we could trust you guys," Angel said, "but you're cool. We'll have a paved runway near the airport for future trips."

In less than twenty minutes on the ground, the crew refueled and loaded the Westwind with six-hundred kilos of pure cocaine produced by Pablo Escobar's Medellin Cartel.

I was relieved there were no gun battles on the ground on this trip, hoped it would be a positive sign for the remainder of the journey. However, the thick, dense fog shrouding the landing strip would be a prelude to a harrowing journey during our return to Long Island.

The ground crew was a happy bunch, evidenced by the number of smiles and thumbs up on taxi and takeoff. We got the impression they were comfortable with their role in the smuggling operation. It was adding millions of dollars to the Colombian economy but causing utter devastation in the United States.

I also had the feeling our partners in crime believed this encounter would be one of many to follow. In the short time we were there, we were not treated as gringos but as part of the outlaw gang. I wanted to limit our exposure on the ground, so we rushed the refueling and loading. The sooner we were airborne, the better.

Or so we thought.

Just after liftoff, disaster struck. The communications and navigation gear, wired through a central control panel, failed again, leaving us with no means of communicating or navigating. To make matters worse, the Caribbean Sea was still overcast, which meant we would get no navigation clues from the ground.

That mattered little as there was only ocean between Colombia and the Caymans, over 600 miles away. Dennis and I agreed our best course of action was to proceed to the Caymans using a rudimentary form of navigation called 'dead-reckoning.'

I hoped the technique would be more reckoning than dead.

Navigating using this method was of limited use as we did not know what direction or speed the wind blew, but it was better than nothing. We DR'd (dead reckoned) our way toward the Caymans, following the aviator's rule in an emergency; first aviate, then navigate, and finally communicate. We didn't have to worry about navigation or communication; we had none. At least we had the GPS coordinates of our start point.

It was about a two-hour flight from Santa Marta to the Caymans, so Dennis and I had plenty of time to discuss our plight. We continued to the Caymans, hoping the undercast would clear and let us see them from some distance. Should that fail, we would spiral down through the undercast, hopeful we would spot the Caymans once we descended below the clouds.

We discarded the possibility of continuing to Cuba or returning to Colombia. We both knew landing in either Cuba or Colombia with a cargo of cocaine aboard would not yield the best result; getting thrown in jail or, in the case of Cuba, tortured for information was not on our to-do list.

It seemed like we had been flying for days as my mind raced in a million directions. Cuba was out, but would a return to a commercial airport in Colombia be

189

the right decision?

We didn't know who we could trust in Colombia. Soon, our option of returning there was off the list; we would not have enough fuel to turn around and fly back. We passed the point of no return. I thought of our chances of surviving a ditching.

Even if we escaped the plane who would rescue us? Nobody knew where we were. I thought about the other times I risked my life and survived. I thought I had finally gone a step too far. If I got out of the airplane after the ditching, I would fight as long as possible to stay alive, despite the slim possibility of rescue. I had been in similar situations before, but none as dire.

If we could not find the Caymans, we would descend below the undercast and conduct a search pattern looking for the islands. If we didn't spot them before we ran out of fuel, we'd ditch the aircraft in the open sea.

Our chances of finding the Caymans after a two-hour flight over open water with no communications or navigation equipment were almost zero. Our chances of surviving a ditching, exiting the aircraft before it sank, and staying alive in the open sea with no flotation or survival equipment were zero.

Interestingly, drowning or being eaten by a shark was preferable to landing in either Colombia or Cuba. We finally arrived at the point where we thought the Caymans would be. There was a hole in the clouds there, allowing us to see the surface. There were no islands, just open sea.

We began a circular descent in the hole, Dennis flying and me looking. As we descended below the level of the clouds, I saw land. I told Dennis to head in that direction. We continued our descent and, as we got closer, Owen Roberts International Airport on Grand Cayman Island appeared with its 7,000 feet of hard-surfaced runway.

A sight for sore eyes.

Dennis and I began a mid-air celebration we soon discovered was a bit premature. We had flown 600 miles over open water with no navigation aids and arrived within 15 miles of our destination. As we flew by the airport tower, we wagged our wings which is the signal for no radio, entered the approach pattern, and landed.

After taxiing to the flight line, we parked the

aircraft, shut down the engines, and exited the cockpit. Two middle-aged gentlemen met us, one in uniform and one in a suit. They were expecting us. DEA in New York alerted officials in the Caymans about the flight.

I thought the gentleman in uniform was a police officer—the Caymans did not have a military—and he carried a gun. He had an islander's accent and sprayed the inside of the aircraft cabin with some aerosol, we later found out was for bugs.

I guess the official was more concerned about bugs than cocaine destined for the U.S. The second gentleman had a British accent which was not unusual since the Cayman Islands was a British protectorate. He was concerned about the avionics problems, and he said he would get right on it. Within seconds a crew of airplane mechanics surrounded the aircraft. We were treated to a snack in the airport lounge and, within two hours, our new friend said we were ready for takeoff.

We took off for the eastern end of Cuba, then would turn north and head for Islip Airport. The weather was clear, and it was an excellent day for flying. While in the Caymans, we checked the weather at Islip. New York. The weather in the Northeast U.S.

was bad and forecast to get worse. We would deal with that problem when it arose.

After the turn, we established ourselves on the correct northerly heading. We had just settled in for the long flight north when the light for the "engine bleed air" illuminated a problem with the right engine. We reviewed the flight manual and procedure. The solution was to shut down the engine; failure to do so would cause a fire.

We shut down the engine.

As with most twin-engine aircraft, the plane would not hold high altitude on one engine. After researching the flight manual's recommendations, we determined that the maximum altitude at our current weight was 16,000 feet. We could not make New York at that altitude as fuel consumption was much higher at 16,000 feet than our planned cruising altitude of 39,000 feet. We did not have sufficient fuel aboard.

We changed our destination to Miami International Airport and requested Miami Center to alert Customs. We also gave them a telephone number for New York Customs. We asked the tower to have Miami Customs inform New York Customs we were now headed for Miami International.

We then informed Miami Center we wanted to leave their frequency for a couple of minutes to check the NOAA weather. While Miami International was clear, there was a line of thunderstorms running north/south between the airport and us. The thunderstorms had reached 22,000 feet and were growing.

We didn't have weather radar aboard, which meant at 16,000 feet—when we penetrated the line of thunderstorms—it would be a roll of the dice whether we hit the heart of a weather cell or smoother air space between cells.

Flying into weather would be challenging with two operating engines; we were operating on one. If we lost the left engine during the Caribbean's flight, we were again reduced to ditching. Provided the aircraft was still in one piece.

We were flying blind into extreme weather, on one engine, carrying enough cocaine to put us in prison for life if we didn't make it to the U.S.

At the moment, taking our chances in the storm was the best of all bad options.

After a long minute and a half of teeth-rattling turbulence, lightning, and rain, we emerged on the other side into clear air. The left engine was still operating normally as we descended into U.S. airspace. We had survived the flight from hell, and the city of Miami was now in our sites.

I notified the tower of our approach, and we were directed to the private aviation section of the airport. We landed safely with only the left engine operating. We touched down on the runway and taxied to the U.S. Customs flight line, where we parked and shut down the remaining engine.

Climbing out of the plane, we were met by a group of Customs agents. I expected a warmer welcome after what we had been through. Then I realized that the Customs agents did not know what we had experienced since leaving New York yesterday.

We had presented ourselves to them with no prior warning, in a broken aircraft carrying a load of illegal drugs, for the Customs Service in New York over 1000 miles away.

The agents' less than enthusiastic welcome was understandable.

Several agents entered the aircraft and searched the interior. As Dennis and I discussed the harrowing flight we had from Colombia, I noticed three agents huddled to the side of the jet. As the agents dispersed, two Customs agents escorted Dennis and me inside and, after a few more questions, left us alone in the room.

I did not have a warm and fuzzy feeling.

Ten minutes passed. Two agents came into the room and took Dennis to another location. More time passed, then another Customs agent came in and asked me if I had a flight bag, to which I replied "no." He left the room, and I was alone again.

During our brief time together, he did not say where Dennis was or what he was doing. However, Dennis had a flight bag, and something didn't feel right. I worried that something was amiss. More time passed, and my worry increased. I tried to recall all of our actions since leaving New York and could identify nothing that would cause the agents any concern.

Finally, some agents came back into the room with Dennis. He was in handcuffs. He said, 'Tell my girlfriend what happened.'"

One Customs agent warned us about talking to

each other and not to do it again. They left the room with Dennis while one agent remained behind and explained to me they had found two kilograms of cocaine in Dennis's flight bag and arrested him.

He was now on his way to jail; I thought this day never end.

The Customs agent left the room, and I was alone again. I was dumbfounded. How could Dennis throw away his opportunity at redemption? I later discovered the U.S. Customs Service would have paid Dennis 75-100,000 dollars for his role in this case. I determined right then my only course of action was to deliver the drugs to Islip as scheduled but in a different Customs aircraft.

When the agents returned, I suggested they transfer the drugs to another plane. I would continue the mission and bring the cargo to West Hampton Airport in Long Island. I was told my role as a pilot for this mission would be taken over by undercover Customs pilots. I had completed the most challenging part of the journey, and now it was out of my hands.

I didn't mention I had seen the aircraft we arrived in for the first time yesterday. Still, I knew that I would have safely completed the journey to New York with an operational aircraft. I waited alone until a Customs agent arrived with a ticket for me from Miami to JFK, New York, and escorted me to the gate. The flight was announced, and I boarded the aircraft and departed. I couldn't believe that it was only yesterday that Dennis and I had left New York.

During the three-hour journey north, I decompressed. My part in this operation was finished. I never did get to see or talk to Dennis again. Much later, I heard they had sent him to prison in Oklahoma.

I didn't know whether Dennis told Customs he had acted alone, or they didn't arrest me because they had no evidence. Either way, I realized how close I had come to being jailed for a crime in which I had no part.

I thought about my life since I had left the Navy and what I should have done differently. It didn't matter. I was where I was and would have to go forward from here. I was forced to start over at 45 years of age and about 150,000 dollars in debt.

Then I thought about the fact that I was actually fortunate. I lived in Europe—where my prison record was unknown—and had an excellent job with a future. My marriage was solid, and my wife and children were in or recently graduated from college. There was little chance that my prison record would surface in the country I lived in because there was no requirement to disclose it.

After the Colombia trip, my account with the U.S. was balanced. I was done with the illegal drug trade on either side of the law, and in the future, I would devote myself to building a stable family and career.

I met Agent Protentis at JFK airport. He arranged a room for me nearby and handed me a ticket to travel to Boston the following day. I explained everything I could recall from the past thirty-six hours and he thanked me for my diligence in completing my most recent mission for the United States.

I told Protentis since Dennis was now in jail, I would contact Novak to arrange delivery of the cocaine. Protentis said that would be a great idea and would contact me if necessary. Protentis dropped me at my hotel and headed back to Long Island.

The Long Island Office put Kenny the Jamaican into this operation to complete the delivery of cocaine to Novak and his associates. I thought my part in the mission was over.

Several months later, Protentis brought me to his office in Boston and, to my complete surprise, paid me fifty thousand dollars in cash for my role in this investigation.

Russ was a man of his word, and because he understood the risks I had taken in this mission, he convinced his bosses to compensate me for my efforts. As a bonus, since I was a citizen of a country that did not require me to claim this money on my income tax, it was all mine.

After lunch and an introduction to his bosses, Protentis took me to Logan International Airport to return to Europe. He and a U.S. Customs Inspector assisted me in completing a declaration form for the $50,000 cash.

He explained the legal requirement to complete the Currency and Monetary Instruments Report walking me through the form. Since I had obtained citizenship abroad, this form would be sent to the IRS and not to my country of residence.

I used my Navy flight training to kill two birds with one stone; I'd redeemed myself in the eyes of

America and also pulled myself further out of debt.

The Controlled Delivery

The Westwind jet arrived in Miami at 4:00 PM with 600 kilos of cocaine on board. Dennis was in jail, Tony was on a commercial flight to New York, and we had only a few recorded conversations with Novak, Krevsky, and their associates.

The U.S. Customs Airwing agreed to transport the cocaine to Long Island in a government-owned jet. We would have to improvise a way to contact Novak that would not cause him to be suspicious, flee New York, and continue his flight from justice.

The cocaine-laden jet lifted off from Miami around 9:30 pm. .

Was Novak aware of the problems which would derail our case? After a few hours of brainstorming, Carbonari and McAndrew said we would discuss the dilemma with Kenny the Jamaican. Novak had given him his pager number several weeks earlier and told him to contact him, so we would have Kenny page him.

Kenny was in a cold sweat in anticipation of the conversation with Novak, and we weren't sure he could pull it off, but he came through in a pinch. He paged Novak from his office and received an immediate return call. Kenny told Novak the aircraft encountered bad weather and some mechanical issues and had to refuel in the Grand Caymans, but they would soon be airborne and headed to Long Island.

Novak sounded a little nervous but relieved. He had been watching the weather channel and was grateful for the update. He told Kenny he had checked into the Holiday Inn near the Westhampton Airport and would have a rental truck sent to transport the "computers" to the hotel. The truck would be parked outside Kenny's office and the keys left under the driver seat.

Novak told Kenny to page him as soon as he contacted the aircraft.

"I want some of the money upfront," Kenny said.

"I'll get you $11,000 when you bring the truck to the hotel, and the rest after the 'computers' were sold."

Kenny agreed, and we were back in the game.

The fog that caused so many problems for the Westwind jet during its flight was now enveloping the entire eastern mid-Atlantic and northeastern seaboard of the United States. It seemed even the weather conspired against us.

The Customs jet was due to arrive at approximately 1:30 A.M., and everything seemed under control. At 2:00 A.M., McAndrew received a telephone call from the U.S. Customs

Airwing. The plane was at Wright Patterson Airforce Base in Ohio and had blown a tire on landing. A military jet would continue the journey with the cargo to Long Island.

Would this payload ever find its way to Westhampton?

At 3:00 AM, we received the answer. Thick fog had overtaken the entire New York area; the military could not land the aircraft anywhere in the region.

Now what?

The gathering of approximately forty federal, state, and local officers lost faith. For the past ten hours, to complicate matters unnecessarily, Mike Nestor hosted media from every major newspaper in the New York region in the conference room of the office. Nestor planned for the media outlets to film the off-load of cocaine from the Westwind jet, exposing the pilots to Pablo Escobar and his associates. Nestor was willing to risk that Dennis and Tony's fate would be the same as Barry Seal for fifteen minutes of fame. I was grateful the thick fog would prohibit news media from filming the off-load.

If the plane ever got here.

Carbonari and McAndrew discussed the latest developments with Assistant U.S. Attorney Ann Kenner. She said that after Kenny received a payment from the crew waiting at the hotel, she would authorize the arrest of the

Krevsky brothers, John Joyce (aka Novak), Rapaport, and anyone else involved at the Holiday Inn.

Arrest teams were organized, and, much to my surprise, I was assigned to a perimeter surveillance team. McAndrew said I should drive my government car and accompany the raid team to the Holiday Inn in Riverhead, New York, but remain on the perimeter because their office had trained a special tactical team for these situations.

Disappointed, but with little choice, I agreed. I emphasized to McAndrew and Carbonari that locating and arresting Novak, because of his fugitive status and as the mastermind of this smuggling operation, was a high priority. He would likely cooperate with our investigation and insulate all of our cooperating sources. They concurred.

At 5:00 AM, agents left the office for their assigned locations. One group would remain at the home of Robert and Daniel Krevsky in Staten Island to execute a federal search warrant and arrest the men if they were home.

A second group would focus on David Rapaport's residence to execute a federal search warrant and make any necessary arrests. A third team would target John Joyce's (Novak's) apartment and execute a federal search warrant. A fourth team would execute arrest warrants for the participants at the Holiday Inn.

205

The arrest signal would be Kenny's return to the rental truck—with his payment—and opening the rental truck rear gate. Two agents would meet Kenny at his office and assist him in recording his conversations with any defendant involved in this investigation.

The weather was worsening by the minute as the fog thickened in the dark of night. At 5:55 A.M., a broadcast was sent out to the team at the hotel that Kenny had spoken to the crew at the hotel and would deliver the truck to the back of the Holiday Inn.

Kenny was told to go to room 112. He would get the $11,000 and then return to the truck with one of the crew to show him the cocaine. Once Kenney opened the door, the arrest team would execute the arrest of the room's occupants and anyone with Kenny.

At 6:00 AM, I saw Kenny and another man open the tailgate, and the raid operation began.

After about ten minutes, I met Carbonari in the hotel lobby, eager to see if the team had Novak in custody. His countenance dropped, "He got away."

Carbonari said the arrest team went in the room's front door while the occupants ran out through sliding glass doors in the back and into the nearby wooded area. The team located three of the four occupants in the woods, but Novak had eluded them. They were returning to the New York State Police Barracks in Nassau County to process the two Colombians and the truck driver.

Carbonari said the fog was so thick in the woods he couldn't see his shoes. He added we would all have a lot of explaining to do. First to Mike Nestor and then to Ann Kenner for allowing this investigation to proceed without arresting Novak for being a wanted federal fugitive from justice.

On the bright side, Carbonari said, Kenny had just spoken to the Krevsky brothers at their home, and agents had placed them under arrest. Rapaport was also in custody.

"Russ, you did a fantastic job," Carbonari said. However, I had a deep feeling of emptiness inside. The fugitive from justice and mastermind of this historical cocaine smuggling operation, and now one of the most-wanted drug smugglers in the United States, was in the wind.

He had beaten me, and I hate to lose. Carbonari said he would meet me back at the New York State Police Barracks in Nassau County. I headed back to my pale blue Ford Crown Victoria, portable radio in hand.

I decided I was not ready to give up. I had not surrendered to the overwhelming odds to bring this operation to a successful conclusion without bringing Novak to justice. I was not a quitter and would not surrender now.

I clipped my portable radio to my belt and, recalling my days as a cub scout, tried to trace a route where Novak might have fled through the densely wooded area. Starting from the room's sliding glass doors at the Holiday Inn, I slowly tracked him into the tree line. The fog hovered about eighteen inches above the ground, clouding my vision. I could only see two or three feet in front of me.

As I trekked through the woods, I came upon a small clearing. Up ahead, I could make out the flashing red lights of a police cruiser as an officer issued a citation to a motorist. I assumed Novak would not have gone that far, or he would have been spotted by the officer.

After searching for at least twenty minutes to no avail, I snapped branches on pine trees and left them hanging as a sign I had passed that location. I headed east in the woods, proceeding slowly between the tree trunks, and came face to face with a medium-sized deer. The deer remained frozen for a moment, as did I, then, in a flash, darted off behind me. I had been detoured off my track, trying to find my original path, when I spotted a pale red object at the base of a small pine tree three or feet in front of me.

My flashlight was almost useless. Maybe it was a jacket dropped by one of the fleeing smugglers?

As I drew a few inches closer, I noticed the rhythmic movement inside what appeared to be a nylon jacket. Was it Novak? Was he armed? Or was it another individual? I turned back to see if the police cruiser's lights were still flashing in the distance. The lights were gone. For the moment, I was alone.

The U.S. Customs Service had a 24-hour mobile radio center in each major region of the United States that could be reached by my portable radio. I could contact them, which Novak would hear, and try to put him at ease by telling the Center I was giving up my search.

After reaching one of the Center employees on the radio, I told him I was returning to the State Police Barracks and terminating my search, which the center acknowledged.

I was now less than two feet from the red jacket wrapped around the base of a tree. I pounced, aiming my right knee on the area I assumed was Novak's neck. He screeched in pain as I shouted, "You so much as flinch, and I will put a round through your skull that will splatter your brains all over the woods."

My knee pressed his neck and head flush into the ground as I grabbed the back of his neck and pressed my revolver against his temple.

"You got me," Novak cried out, "don't shoot!"

I lowered my body, pressing my knee into his tailbone, and told him to place both hands behind his back as I patted him down. He complied, and I put my handcuffs on his wrists.

"Are you armed?" I asked.

"No,"

I did find a knife on the ground near his legs, which I stashed in my back pocket.

"Are you John Novak?"

"No, I am John Joyce."

"Are you alone?"

"Yeah."

I brought him to his feet, grabbed the handcuffs tightly by the short chain between his wrists, then I realized I had no idea where I was. However, I knew Novak had run straight to that location, so I would retrace his steps. As the fog dissipated, I could see the Holiday Inn sign illuminated in the distance.

I found my Crown Victoria in the mist and unlocked the driver's side door. Knowing that Novak was facing a twenty-year sentence on his case in California and a possible life sentence for his role in this case, I was not taking any chance he would attempt to escape. I popped the trunk of the vehicle and gently placed him inside.

Starting my vehicle, I pulled over to the public phone in the parking lot, placing a call to Dave McAndrew at the Nassau County State Police Barracks, asking for an update on the case.

He said he was taking "a lot of heat" because Novak escaped, and the bosses were enraged. McAndrew said I would have to call the bosses in Boston to calm them down. I told him I would meet him in less than ten minutes, and I wanted to discuss something with him in person. McAndrew said he would wait for me out in front of the barracks.

When I arrived, McAndrew met me at my vehicle and I told him I had collected some equipment left behind at the Holiday Inn. As I opened the trunk, I watched as he broke into a smile from ear to ear.

"You son of a bitch" he said. "My guys lost him, and you covered our asses." McAndrew and I brought Novak into the State Police Barracks for prisoner booking. Carbonari, who was smiling for the first time in three months, met us at the top of the stairs. He said my supervisor, Jim Burke, had been calling Mike Nestor for an update on the investigation and wanted to speak with me.

Carbonari and I took Novak into an interview room and read him his rights. I showed him a booking photograph from San Diego. His face fell.

"Sure looks like you, Mr. Joyce."

"That's me; I'm John Novak."

"You are looking at life in prison. Do you want a lawyer?"

"I am done running; I want to cooperate."

Carbonari looked him straight in the eyes and banged on the table. "You tell one lie, and you will never get out of prison."

Novak nodded, "I won't."

Carbonari escorted Novak to the booking area. Dave McAndrew stopped me in the hallway.

"I'll go with Carbonari. You need to call your boss. He's called five times looking for you."

I finally returned a call to my supervisor, Jim Burke. He told me he had talked to Mike Nestor who filled him in on the arrests, Novak's status as a fugitive, and his escape.

I told Burke Novak's escape was short-lived. I'd found him in the woods, and he was being fingerprinted as we spoke. Burke said the Regional Director, Haig Sohegian, was traveling and wanted to extend congratulations to me on the case's success.

"Have him call me directly," I said.

"We're at a conference in Canada," he answered.

"They can call me anytime," I replied. "You should have

let me work the case in Boston to learn about narcotics smuggling instead of attending those dog and pony shows."

Burke was speechless; I hung up the telephone. I'd made my point on the politics of spineless case management.

While pondering the success of this investigation, I had mixed emotions of joy and sadness.

Mostly, the results were beyond compare. However, I had an emptiness in my heart. A year of work from my first encounters with Dennis and Tony to the largest seizure of cocaine from a private aircraft in U.S. history was now finished.

Dennis was in jail, Tony was headed back to a solid career, and I would have to start all over again. Dennis had the trust of members of the Mafia in Boston interested in transporting narcotics by airplane into the U.S. Was there a way to keep the negotiations Dennis had started with Rizzo going?

The following day, I discussed this issue with Assistant United States Attorney (AUSA) Kenner. She told me if the defendants go to trial, my testimony would be central to the prosecution's case. I told her I was prepared to assist in any way required.

I asked what her thoughts were on keeping Dennis on the street until he could introduce another pilot to Rizzo and his associates. Kenner said that convincing the U.S. Attorney's Office in Miami to agree would be an uphill battle, but she would discuss it with them.

One by one, she arranged for the defendants to be brought from the Manhattan Correctional Institute to her office and interviewed by Carbonari and myself.

It was clear from the outset—because of the overwhelming evidence—the conspirators would be pleading guilty on all counts.

The entire crew would cooperate with our investigation in exchange for favorable recommendations at their sentencing in federal court. Novak signed a plea agreement pledging his cooperation with investigators and the pending case against him in California.

On my way to one of the conference room interviews, after a brief conversation with AUSA Kenner, she introduced me to the United States Attorney for the Southern District of New York, Rudolph Giuliani.

Mr. Giuliani thanked me for my part in the investigation and diligence in pursuing this case from its beginning to a successful conclusion. Mr. Giuliani went on to become the Mayor of New York City. He is an attorney for Donald J. Trump.

Watch Your Back

My job in New York was done. I would return to the Boston office to develop more sources in smuggling investigations.

I arrived at the Boston office the following Monday, back to answering duty agent calls and being asked to assist other, more politically connected agents on investigative leads given them by my supervisor.

The Boston office hierarchy had a small select group of agents being groomed for success despite their lack of experience. I was not in that group and would be relegated to assisting in advancing their careers.

My new supervisor, Jim Scott, often questioned how I developed high-level informants in the Long Island case. He asked why I was still trying to use Dennis, who had tried to take two kilograms from the cargo on the Westwind jet.

I told him Dennis could still prove to be a valuable asset in an air smuggling investigation. I sensed there was an ulterior motive but could not put my finger on it. I would soon be enlightened on my suspicions.

Most agents in the office had no clue about the tireless effort required to complete an investigation of this magnitude. On several occasions, I was asked if I had received a "hot tip" about the jet from Colombia.

My answer was sarcastic. "I saw a Colombian at the airport drop his suitcase. A bunch of kilo bricks of cocaine broke open on the floor, and some white powder came out. At first, I thought it was sugar."

In early July, Scott called me into his office. He told me that the Miami Office had requested my presence to prepare for Dennis's criminal case. He said the U.S. Attorney's Office required specific information on my cultivation of Dennis as a source. Scott said the Miami Office would fund the travel for my trip. I was to travel there the following week for an appointment at 1:00 PM on Monday with the AUSA handling the case.

I had heard that Tech Operations Officer John Murray was now assigned to Miami. I contacted him to see if he was available to meet me upon my arrival in Miami. He agreed and said he would book me a room in the Grand Hyatt Hotel.

I was not excited about traveling to Miami during a hot, humid summer, but my presence was required. I stepped out of the American Airlines Terminal at noontime, and before I got to the curb, I was drenched in sweat. The air was oppressive, and I now realized why people do not travel to

Miami in July.

Murray was waiting for me. I threw my bag in his car, and we were off to the United States Attorney's Office. John was very business-like and warned me of the peril I was facing in Miami.

Murray said my office in Boston contacted the Miami Office of Internal Affairs regarding my relationship with Dennis. He said I would be questioned by the prosecuting attorney about my willingness to assist in Dennis's prosecution. I told Murray it was my job to put smugglers in jail, and I was prepared to do my best.

Murray said the Boston office, and especially my supervisor Jim Scott, felt differently. Murray also said the case agent on Dennis's arrest was Pat Roche, who had recently transferred to the Office of Investigations from the Office of Internal Affairs. It would be his duty to find holes in my statements.

I was dumbfounded and confused but not surprised. Murray told me Dennis had a bail reduction hearing scheduled the following day, and my testimony might be required. Also, Murray said my testimony might be necessary, and I should tell AUSA Lee Bentley precisely what I told him.

That, of course, was always my intention.

Upon arrival at the federal courthouse, Murray and I were directed to a small conference room in the U.S. Attorney's Public Corruption Unit. Inside the room, I was introduced to Assistant U.S. Attorney Alan Sullivan from the Major Crimes division, Lee Bentley, the AUSA prosecuting Dennis, and U.S. Customs Special Agent Pat Roche.

Murray and I sat in the two empty seats next to Roche, on the opposite side of the table from Sullivan and Bentley. Then things took an ominous turn.

Roche asked me if I knew Dennis had tried to smuggle two kilos of cocaine from Colombia secreted in his flight bag.

"Yes, I was."

Sullivan asked me if I would have searched Dennis and his flight bag if the Westwind jet had successfully landed in Long Island.

"It was agency policy that Tony and Dennis be thoroughly searched upon their arrival," I said.

Sullivan asked if I would be the one to search Dennis since I had developed him.

"I was not sure who would have searched him," I answered, "but somebody would have."

Sullivan reiterated Dennis had attempted to smuggle the two kilos of cocaine and told the arresting agents Tony was not aware of his intentions. The investigators believed that Dennis and Tony were truthful. Roche said he was curious why Dennis would smuggle the cocaine.

"I knew Dennis had been treated for cocaine addiction in the past," I said, "but that he seemed to put that behind him. Also, several other agents and I in Long Island told Dennis he would be eligible for a significant cash award if the case was successful."

Bentley asked me how much Dennis might receive for his information and cooperation.

"Per agency guidelines, he might be eligible for up to one hundred thousand dollars."

Sullivan asked me if Dennis was ever promised this award.

"He was never promised anything, only that per his source agreement, he might be eligible if he was fully cooperative throughout the investigation."

Roche asked me if Dennis told me he had planned to smuggle two kilograms of cocaine and if I would cooperate in Dennis's federal prosecution.

This unveiled the true meaning behind this interrogation, but I was determined not to let them rattle me.

"Of course not. I was not aware of Dennis's intentions, and I am fully prepared to assist in his federal prosecution."

219

Sullivan asked if I had become too close to Dennis.

They had crossed a line from case preparation into me being a target of an investigation.

"Should I have an attorney present? I do not appreciate the tone of these questions." I got up and walked out of the conference room door.

Sullivan stopped me in the hallway and said that he was only trying to understand my relationship with Dennis. He said my supervisor in the Boston office told him I had become too friendly with Dennis.

Also, the Boston office told him I brought Dennis to my home and taken him to social functions by myself. I told Sullivan those assertions were false, and my supervisor was a liar.

Sullivan then asked me to return to the conference room and detail my cultivation of such a high-level source. After I regained my composure, I told Sullivan that in my career as a federal agent with ATF and the U.S. Customs Office of Investigations, I had the knack and tenacity to pursue investigative leads and develop upper echelon sources of information.

I told him I obtained a list of airplane pilots, fishing boat owners, and boat captains residing in New England on federal probation or parole. I placed their names on a lookout list for international arrivals in the U.S. Customs Treasury Enforcement System (TECS). I also told Sullivan that in April 1987, I received an alert in TECS that Dennis and Tony had entered the United States as the pilots onboard a private aircraft landing in San Juan, Puerto Rico on a flight from the Dominican Republic. Then I received a photocopy of their U.S. Customs declaration forms with their dates of birth and addresses.

I laid out the complete process. From contacting their federal probation officer to getting his permission to use the technical violation to gain their cooperation to the full report I made to the United States Federal Probation Office.

Sullivan asked if I could provide AUSA Lee Bentley with a copy of these monthly status reports. I gave him my room number at the Grand Hyatt and told him they were in the safe in my hotel room.

Pat Roche, without saying a word got up and left the room. Sullivan said he and Bentley would further review the case. The bail reduction hearing for Dennis was scheduled for 1:00 PM the following day. He wanted to meet with me one hour before to review my testimony.

Murray and I left the U.S. Attorney Office. I was visibly shaken. It's one thing to face scrutiny on your case management and preparations. It's a whole other animal when it's obvious you've become the innocent target of a disinformation campaign.

Murray said he was surprised Alan Sullivan, who was temporarily assigned to the U.S. Attorney's Office of Public Corruption, was in the meeting along with Pat Roche. Roche's background was Internal Affairs, not criminal investigations.

I told him I thought the Boston office was trying to tarnish my integrity and wanted Sullivan to do the dirty work. Murray agreed and said Pat Roche was probably stoking the flames. Murray dropped me at my hotel, and I rode the elevator to my floor.

It was now early in the evening. I entered my room, collapsed on the bed, and watched the ceiling fan slowly rotate. Was this the end of my career? Was the chief prosecutor for public corruption preparing to indict me for my part in a conspiracy to smuggle two kilos of cocaine into the U.S.?

I was a member of the Federal Law Enforcement Officers Association and had twenty-four-hour access to their attorneys. I spoke to Larry Berger, one of their lead attorneys. He counseled me to contact him if Sullivan requested to interview me again and said he would get an attorney in Miami to represent me in such an instance.

I continued to stare at the ceiling fan and was startled by the room telephone. I answered and was shocked to hear Lee Bentley's voice on the other end. He said he was finishing in his office and wanted to meet me for a beer to discuss the case. I said that I didn't feel comfortable and suggested he meet me in the pool. He laughed and said he would buy me a beer in the lobby, and I could pat him down for a wire. I paused for a moment and agreed to meet him.

I took a quick shower, changed, and headed down to the lobby. Bentley entered through the revolving door. As we shook hands, I put my left hand on the small of his back.

"Russ, I told you I would not be wearing a wire."

"Yeah," I said, "but after the interview with Sullivan, I'm careful."

He told me he had just finished a long meeting with Sullivan. He said Sullivan did nothing but rave about me and how I had developed a case of historical proportions from nothing, with tenacity and perseverance.

Bentley also told me Sullivan chewed out Pat Roche and his supervisor at Customs for wasting his time. Bentley said the only air smuggling cases Customs agents bring to his office occur when a plane crash lands in the water or into a building.

I laughed.

Bentley was a gentleman. I could tell he was remorseful about the entire scenario with Pat Roche and my office in Boston. He asked if there was anything he or Sullivan could do for me. I saw my chance. I asked if, after Dennis plead guilty to smuggling charges, his office would stay the date Dennis would report to federal prison. I needed his cooperation with me on Anthony Rizzo and his Mafia associates. Bentley said I should discuss the issue with Sullivan, who had Boston roots and could support my request.

*****

It was another steamy day in Miami. I entered the federal courthouse, hopeful this day would differ significantly from the previous one. AUSA Bentley and Sullivan greeted me in the reception area of the U.S. Attorney's Office.

Sullivan said Bentley would be preparing for Dennis's bail hearing and wanted to meet with me in his office. Sullivan said that he had discussed my request with the first AUSA of the criminal division about Dennis. He had his blessing to work something out to keep Dennis on the street and under my supervision until he had completed his work with me.

Dennis would have to plead guilty to his attempt to

smuggle two kilograms of cocaine into Miami. While awaiting a date to report to federal prison, he could continue to assist me in any investigation before sentencing. Sullivan said Dennis's attorney agreed with this scenario, and the plea agreement for him was being finalized. Sullivan apologized for his approach the previous day and wished me good luck in my career.

In July of 1988, Dennis pled guilty U.S. District Court in Miami to smuggling charges. His sentencing date would be delayed until December of 1988, which gave him approximately five months to earn a reduction in his sentence duration for his cooperation. Dennis would serve his sentence at the federal correctional institute in Raybrook, New York. The site of the 1980 Winter Olympics Village converted into a secure federal prison.

The next few months were like déjà vu. Dennis worked his magic with Rizzo, who introduced him to mob enforcer William "Red" Brady. Brady and Rizzo had questions about Dennis's arrest in Miami, which had reached the local Boston newspapers.

Dennis told Brady and Rizzo that one of the Customs agents had stolen the cocaine, and most charges would be dismissed except for an 18-month sentence for a federal parole violation. Brady said that a major player with contacts in Mexico and Colombia wanted to meet Dennis.

The following day, Brady met Dennis in Boston. I watched them as they drove to Wonderland Dog Track in Revere, MA, where Brady introduced Dennis to Jack. Jack was an imposing figure, approximately 6"4" and a solid 220 lbs., who boasted of many connections in Mexico and wanted to move planeloads of marijuana to Texas. The conversation which I recorded was loud and clear. I was in the game again.

Dennis, and another source I developed, would help me build a case against Jack, which would lead me to the Cali Cocaine Cartel in Colombia. It would become the most significant narcotics distribution network in the world.

I focused on building my next case and left the office politics to the others. I didn't have time to waste on such nonsense.

News Headline from Cocaine Seizure

NEW YORK - U.S. Customs said its record $8 million seizure of cocaine in New York this week came about when their undercover operatives learned the suspects were attempting to get a jet aircraft to transport a quantity of cocaine from Colombia to Long Island, N.Y.

Customs said the chief suspect in the mega-bust, Robert Krevsky, who was previously arrested for a smuggling attempt in 1983, began a series of negotiations with Customs undercover operatives to obtain the aircraft and assist in the logistics of the smuggling attempt.

The agency then said Mr. Krevsky, along with co-conspirators, obtained a Westwind I jet aircraft leased by Hercules Construction Company of Brooklyn, N.Y., for $40,000 per month, from Westlease Aircraft, a Delaware corporation.

After the jet traveled from New York to Colombia and was loaded with cocaine it proceeded back to the U.S. but lost an engine and made an emergency landing in Miami.

Flight of the Westwind

Acknowledgments

The author would like to acknowledge the invaluable contribution of U.S. Customs Sector Communication personnel in Boston and New York. This case's success, and almost every case conducted by U.S. Customs, would not have been possible without their dedication to duty.

My friends Bernie, Joe, Ed, Ludo, Ellen, Carmen, Judy, and others all did an outstanding job of connecting me with my pilots who would call collect or the 800-number sector at any hour. They would keep them on hold until I could, in turn, call in from a public phone to be connected (patched through in our terms) to each other. They were my dear friends at all hours of the night, obtaining registry listing on license plates and tracking me down on my voice pager wherever I might be. I could not have completed this investigation without their tireless and selfless efforts.

228

About the Author

Retired Senior Special Agent Russell Protentis is the eldest of four sons. His mother, Inga, is a Nazi German Holocaust survivor, and his father, Sam, is a wounded World War II veteran. Protentis graduated Magna Cum Laude from Northeastern University. At school, he met his wife Lynda, now married 41 years, and raised five successful adults.

In 1976, Protentis began his career in federal law enforcement with the Bureau of Alcohol, Tobacco, and Firearms, and in 1982 transferred to the U.S. Customs Service Office of Investigations, which, after 9/11, merged with the U.S. Immigration and Naturalization Service to become U.S. Immigration and Customs Enforcement. During his tenure at U.S. Customs Office of Investigations, he became a renowned expert in air smuggling investigations.

Between 1988 and 1991, he cultivated several high-level informants and airplane pilots who infiltrated both the Medellin and Cali, Colombia Cocaine Cartels. He conducted numerous air smuggling investigations of historic proportions resulting in the arrest of more than thirty individuals, including key leaders of both cartels, the largest seizure of cocaine from a private aircraft in U.S. Customs

Service history, the confiscation of more than 10,000 pounds of cocaine, two million dollars cash, and over 10 million dollars in assets including a Westwind 1 jet aircraft.

The successful air smuggling investigation in this book was the first-ever initiated by the U.S. Customs Service north of Florida. During the same period, Protentis cultivated and directed an informant who penetrated a marijuana smuggling organization. The cases resulted in the arrest of eleven individuals and the seizure of a fishing vessel en route from Colombia containing 20,000 lbs of marijuana and one million dollars in cash and assets.

In 1999, Protentis worked as the undercover agent on an investigation involving Chinese Nationals resulting in the arrest and conviction of two individuals for attempting to export missile technology to China. This investigation received international acclaim because the U.S. Secretary of State was in negotiations with the Chinese Government to amend a treaty on Weapons Technology exchange between the U.S. and China. Protentis, as the case agent and undercover operative, conducted a clandestine meeting in Europe with Iranian Military Officials. The investigation resulted in thwarting their attempt to procure military equipment from the United States.

While with Immigration and Customs Enforcement and

after 9/11, Protentis worked in an undercover capacity on an International Arms Export investigation of a Pakistani military officer. The officer wanted to procure missile technology from the U.S. to be sold to Al Qaeda terrorists, which lead to his conviction and deportation from the U.S.

In 2006, while assigned to the DEA, Protentis received the U.S. Justice Department's award for "Outstanding Contribution in Drug Law Enforcement" from United States Attorney General Alberto Gonzales.

During his 33-year career as a federal agent, Protentis was also selected for temporary assignment to the U.S. Secret Service to provide candidate protection during eight Presidential Election Campaigns. These assignments involved security details of six current or former Presidents of the United States and the 2002 Winter Olympic Games in Salt Lake City, Utah.

Protentis now operates a seafood processing plant in Oman that exports products to the United States and Southeast Asia. He is also a former Deacon of his church, a grandfather, and is actively involved in national politics.

About JEBWizard Publishing

JEBWizard Publishing offers a hybrid approach to publishing. By taking a vested interest in your book's success, we put our reputation on the line to create and market a quality publication. We offer a customized solution based on your individual project needs.

Our authors' catalog spans the spectrum of fiction, non-fiction, Young Adult, True Crime, Self-help, and Children's books.

Contact us for submission guidelines at

https://www.jebwizardpublishing.com

Info@jebwizardpublishing.com

Or in writing at

JEBWizard Publishing
37 Park Forest Rd.
Cranston, RI 02920

CPSIA information can be obtained
at www.ICGtesting.com
Printed in the USA
BVHW071143200421
605409BV00013B/319

9 781736 214626